TRIUMPH AT KAPYONG

To my parents

TRIUMPH AT KAPYONG

CANADA'S PIVOTAL BATTLE IN KOREA

DAN BJARNASON

FOREWORDS BY ADRIENNE CLARKSON
AND PETER MANSBRIDGE

DUNDURN
TORONTO

Editor: Jennifer McKnight
Design: Courtney Horner
Printer: Webcom

Library and Archives Canada Cataloguing in Publication

Bjarnason, Dan
    Triumph at Kapyong : Canada's pivotal battle
in Korea / Dan Bjarnason.

Includes bibliographical references and index.
ISBN 978-1-55488-872-6

    1. Korean War, 1950-1953--Campaigns--Korea (South)--
Kap¬y'ong-gun. 2. Canada. Canadian Army--History--Korean
War, 1950-1953. 3. Canada. Canadian Army. Princess Patricia's
Canadian Light Infantry--History. 4. Korean War, 1950-1953--
Canada. I. Title.

DS918.2.K36B53 2011   951.904'242   C2010-907733-4

1   2   3   4   5   15   14   13   12   11

We acknowledge the support of the **Canada Council for the Arts** and the **Ontario Arts Council** for our publishing program. We also acknowledge the financial support of the **Government of Canada** through the **Canada Book Fund** and **Livres Canada Books**, and the **Government of Ontario** through the **Ontario Book Publishers Tax Credit** program, and the **Ontario Media Development Corporation**.

Care has been taken to trace the ownership of copyright material used in this book. The author and the publisher welcome any information enabling them to rectify any references or credits in subsequent editions.

J. Kirk Howard, President

Printed and bound in Canada.
www.dundurn.com

Dundurn Press
3 Church Street, Suite 500
Toronto, Ontario, Canada
M5E 1M2

Gazelle Book Services Limited
White Cross Mills
High Town, Lancaster, England
LA1 4XS

Dundurn Press
2250 Military Road
Tonawanda, NY
U.S.A. 14150

CONTENTS

Foreword

by Adrienne Clarkson

As a child, the Korean War was a very significant event for me. After arriving in Canada as refugees and struggling to find our place in Canada during the war time and right after it, my family was very alert to the idea that things were still in flux in China. Mao Zedong had triumphed in 1949, and my father announced solemnly to us that we would never be returning to Hong Kong. We were going to become Canadian, and the door was shut forever on our past. As a result of the Japanese conquering Hong Kong in 1941, we had lived under the occupation for six months, and then, in a dramatic and now unbelievable way, were rescued and made our way to Canada of which we had only flimsy knowledge and where my father had some business connections.

Every evening in our cottage at McGregor Lake, we huddled by the radio and listened to the news. My father was very pessimistic about General MacArthur being able to hang on to Korea in the face of the Chinese offensive. He would say, "We're just going to be pushed right off the end of that peninsula, right off the end of Busan." Every day was full of punishing news. As a family, we were extremely depressed. It wasn't that we wanted to return to Hong Kong; it was the idea that somehow defeat was coming again.

Meanwhile, I personally felt a connection with the war because my friend Ruth Gray, whose father was the minister at St. Paul's Church on Daily Avenue in Ottawa, had seen her brother, Alex, go off as a private with the Princess Patricia's 2nd Battalion. He was killed and we plunged into a deep mourning — all of his former classmates at Lisgar Collegiate, the parish of St. Paul's, and the group of giggling girlfriends who shared lunch in one corner of the cafeteria. Alex was a grand young man and we worshiped him as only young teenagers can do to someone who plays football wonderfully and who volunteers to go to a war. Ruth herself died several years ago and we had been in touch since I mentioned her brother several times while I was governor general and commander-in-chief. He will always be, for me, the living embodiment of a spirit of gallantry and devil-may-care commitment.

When I gave the commander-in-chief's commendation to the 2nd Battalion for their actions in Medak Pocket in 2003, I thought of Alex. When I spoke at the funeral of our four 3rd Battalion soldiers killed in the friendly fire incident in 2002, I thought of Alex. And when I visited the 2nd Battalion at Shilo, Manitoba, in May 2010, I again thought of Alex.

As colonel-in-chief of the Princess Patricia's Canadian Light Infantry since 2007, I am completely bound up with the fortunes and the lives of this extraordinary regiment. The Patricias are the stuff that legends are made of: raised swiftly at the outbreak of the First World War; distinguishing themselves at Vimy Ridge, Canada's defining battle; and culminating in Ortona in the Second World War — all of these are lights on a path of beauty, sacrifice, and honour.

I am very proud that Dan Bjarnason has written the history of the Battle of Kapyong, in which the Korean Special Force and 2 PPCLI play such an important role. It is a thrilling account, and though I have particular reasons to remember the name Kapyong, I am very aware that most Canadians do not remember it. For the first time, the moving story of Major Levy, in which I played a marginal personal role, is revealed in its sad complexity. This is history at its finest. I am also fortunate to know people like Hub Gray (Captain Retired); Bjarnason draws very much on Hub's own memoir entitled *Beyond the Danger Close*.

When I am with my regiment, I know that they incarnate the true spirit of the Patricias, who are "first in the field" and who have such a close relationship as officers and men because of the kind of infantry regiment it has always been.

Anyone going to Korea today, seeing that hilly countryside and the magnificent forests that cover it, would find it difficult to believe what

I saw in the newsreels when I was a child in 1950–51: Korean peasants digging through the earth and eating roots and what looked like bark from trees; the hills almost completely denuded except for a few leafless shrubs. We sacrificed in order for that to change and we should feel some satisfaction now, knowing that South Korea has developed so strongly as an industrial power. If we were sacrificing in order to bring a better way of life, we certainly did it successfully in Korea. Our loss of 520 are buried in the U.N. Memorial Park cemetery in Busan.

The Battle of Kapyong is an enthralling story of "they shall not pass" dimensions. Our small band of seven hundred stood off an enemy of five thousand tough soldiers who had just been through a triumphant revolution. The word *Kapyong* is synonymous with courage. All Canadians can be proud.

The Right-Honourable Adrienne Clarkson, PC, CC, CMM, CD
Twenty-seventh Governor General of Canada

Foreword

by Peter Mansbridge

There's a small plastic container on a shelf in my office at the CBC in Toronto. Most people don't even notice it. I do. Almost every day.

Dan Bjarnason brought it to me in April of 1992, just after he'd arrived home from an overseas assignment. He had travelled across the ocean to report on half a dozen First World War veterans who had fought at one of the most important battles in Canadian military history — the battle of Vimy Ridge. They'd returned to the same spot, seventy-five years on, to honour the 3,598 Canadians who died on that ridge, in a battle that helped define us as a nation. Vimy Ridge is hallowed ground, and the stunning Walter Allward monument that looms over the area is testament to the first time Canadians had fought under Canadian command.

So what's in the container? And why do I cherish it to this day? Dan knew that as an amateur military history buff myself, I had envied his assignment. I'd never been to Vimy Ridge and desperately wished I had. So Dan did the next best thing — he brought Vimy Ridge to me. He scooped up a small amount of Vimy soil, placed it inside a 35mm camera film capsule, brought it back across the ocean, and placed it on my desk. Every once and a while I do more than just look at that old capsule — I open it and touch the particles inside. Touching history.

Over the years I've added a few other little containers to the collection Dan started for me: sand from Juno Beach in Normandy, gravel from Apeldoorn in the Netherlands, a stone from Hong Kong. All encourage me, again, to touch history.

Which brings me to this book. It's written by my friend and colleague of almost forty years, that same Dan Bjarnason. The conflict in Korea in the early 1950s and Canada's role in it has been called the "Forgotten War," and for the most part that description is correct. So few Canadians know what happened, why it happened, and how our own soldiers fought and died there.

That near amnesia over Korea is surprising given the enormous strategic importance and dreadful scale of the conflict in which, for three years, communist forces of North Korea and China slugged it out with U.S. and U.N. contingents in what famed American military historian S.L.A. Marshall called "The century's nastiest little war."

For all frontline troops in the war, including Canadian, U.S., British, and various U.N. troops, as well as those on the communist side, the term "little" would not have come easily to mind. It was an enormous bloodbath involving Chinese mass human-wave attacks and ferocious artillery duels that saw a pace of battle deaths that far outstripped even the subsequent Vietnam War.

It was in this landscape of mountain trenches, dugouts, and steel defences in Korea that Canadian troops made their mark through repelling Chinese troop attacks and in repeated patrolling into no man's land. They fought largely within a famously steady Commonwealth Division made up of British, Australian, Canadian, and New Zealand troops. Canadian "volunteers" sailed off to Korea without illusions about war. A great many were veterans of the Second World War, and their ranks contained, according to historian Desmond Morton, "plenty of rough diamonds with battle experience."

All their toughness would be required for a war remembered by veterans not only for bitter fighting, but for a relentlessly harsh climate, where one baked in summer and froze in winter, and where the terrain of one mountain range flowed into another, seemingly designed to make war impossible for armour, and hellish on infantry.

It was a lonely conflict. Troops felt cut off from home, and served without the kind of intense and united popular support that had bolstered Second World War troops. And over this very "hot" war there hung a curtain of Cold War terror almost unimaginable today. The U.S. talked openly of the possibility of using nuclear weapons to end fighting, while China hinted as broadly of its ability to flood Korea with up to a million fresh troops.

The war resulted in a partial victory for the West, as the aggression was stopped and thereafter contained. But there was little celebrating once the fighting was over, and returning troops never received the debt of gratitude their countries owed them.

Instead, the very nightmarish quality of the Korean War caused western societies to push it well into the background of thought, where it remains to this day.

No one, and certainly not Canadians, should forget the sacrifices of the past. For me those little capsules containing the soil where some of our most famous military moments took place help do that. For all of us, this book can now do the same for a part of our proud history so many of us know virtually nothing about. That is so wrong. Those who never came home from a fight we asked them to conduct on our behalf deserve better from their country.

Read on, and touch history. Our history.

Peter Mansbridge

ACKNOWLEDGEMENTS

Thanks for their candour, patience, and insights goes to Kapyong veterans Charles Petrie, Kim Reynolds, Rollie Lapointe, Al Lynch, John Bishop, Mike Czuboka, Don Hibbs, Murray Edwards, Bill Chrysler, Alex Sim, Smiley Douglas, Bob Menard, Bill White, Bernie Cote, Ron Rushton, and Hub Gray, who has donated many of his Korean War photographs to the PPCLI Archives and Museum in Calgary and his personal Kapyong documents and letters to the Military Museums, Library and Archives, University of Calgary.

And special thanks for their special guidance and help to: Colonel Walt Ford, United States Marine Corps; William Johnson, Historian, Department of National Defence; military scholars David Bercuson and Jack Granatstein; Marjorie Levy; Don Levy; Korean veteran and war artist Ted Zuber; Maggie Arbour-Doucette, Jane Naisbitt, and Susan Ross of the Canada War Museum; Dora Winter of Library and Archives Canada; John Wright and Donna Zambory of Military Museums, Library and Archives, University of Calgary; military author and historian Mark Zuehlke; Vince Courtenay of the Korea Veterans Association of Canada; and Korean War PPCLI veteran and journalist, Peter Worthington.

Ivan Duguay, a Canadian who lectures at Semyung University in South Korea, has made a hobby of exploring the battlefield and his descriptions of Kapyong today provide a great sense of place.

My editor at Dundurn Press, Jennifer McKnight, turned what I feared could have been an agonizing process into a delightfully pleasant and smooth collaboration.

Also appreciation to PPCLI Regimental Major Harpel Mandaher, and to Regimental Adjutant Captain Richard Dumas in Edmonton for making available many photographs from the PPCLI archives, and also the Kapyong article by Lieutenant Colonel Owen Browne.

Much gratitude to friends and former colleagues at the CBC: Eric Foss, Manmeet Ahluwalia, and Peter Mansbridge.

Adrienne Clarkson took a deep personal interest in this story, which is reflected in her touching foreword.

Susan Papp started it all rolling by introducing me to the people at Dundurn Press, who took to the Kapyong story from the start.

When the author was an officer cadet at the School of Infantry in Camp Borden Ontario in the early 1960s, his platoon commander was Lieutenant Don Ardelian, a distinguished PPCLI veteran of the fighting in Korea. It was Ardelian who first planted the seeds of the Kapyong story, a half century ago. He died in June 2010.

And finally, and especially, to Nance who's been pleading with me for years to write this story, and had faith in the Kapyong tale long before I was convinced there was such a thrilling tale to tell.

INTRODUCTION

Kapyong is the perfect example of the perfectly fought defensive battle.

It is a thrilling story, but is now largely an invisible battle from the "Forgotten War" in Korea six decades ago. It is about as far removed from us as the Second World War was from the Riel Rebellion. *Kapyong* is about one April night in 1951, when freshly minted, hopelessly outnumbered Canadian soldiers made a desperate stand on a rocky hill near a nothing village on the edge of nowhere.

Korea was largely a war at night, in small groups, fought to grab control of hilltops. It was a war of patrols and ambushes; of snipers and prisoner snatches. There were no Vimy Ridges here, or Normandys. In Korea, Canadians usually died in little batches of fives and sixes. But not always. Sometimes there were awful battles where positions were swamped by Chinese human-wave attacks. Kapyong was one such terrible fight. It was Canada's first battle in the Korean War.

This is the story of only 700 men, all volunteers, in the 2nd Battalion of Princess Patricia's Canadian Light Infantry, who'd signed up specifically to fight, and fight specifically, in Korea. The story is about how on this lonely night they found themselves surrounded and cut off by 5,000 tough, seasoned Chinese veterans sweeping around their positions.

It was a terrifying battle-in-the-dark that had the feel of a Canadian Thermopylae; the several hundred against the several thousand; with hand-to-hand fighting with bayonets, shovels, and rifle butts when ammunition and grenades ran out; with foxholes lost and retaken; and with calling down artillery fire on their own positions.

Kapyong is also about what *did not* happen. The Canadian position held on, despite everything. The hill did not fall. The Korean capital, Seoul, only a few miles away, was not laid open to a Chinese breakthrough. The Chinese assault was blunted and led to nowhere. And so, the Korean War did not end abruptly in April 1951 in a communist victory.

It's a matter of some resentment to Canadian soldiers who came later to the war that it is Kapyong that resonates. No one now gives a second thought to the other awful battles that followed, where Canadians fought and died in human-wave attacks just like those at Kapyong; places with drab names like Hill 419, Hill 532, Hill 355, Hill 97, or Hill 187. But, however unfairly, no one remembers any of this now. It is Kapyong that has captured the popular memory of what little is recalled of our war in Korea.

There is only room for one event that symbolizes a country's wartime experience. For the Russians, among a thousand battles against the Nazis, it is surely Stalingrad. For the British, in their years upon years of fighting Napoleon, it is Waterloo, and also, perhaps, Trafalgar, though no one ever talks about "meeting your Trafalgar." For Americans, the iconic Iwo Jima flag-raising on a South Pacific flyspeck has come to stand for their entire Second World War experience.

And so it is Kapyong that is Canada's singular Korean War memory.

As sailors in the Royal Navy must have felt the hand of Nelson or Drake on their shoulder during the darkest days of the war against the U-boats, it is knowing of past heroism and sacrifice that sustains generations that follow through the most fearsome hours and blackest nights. That is why "tradition," so quaint a concept to many civilians, is so priceless to armies. If scarcely any civilian now has ever heard of Kapyong, every Canadian soldier in today's army surely knows of it and what happened there. Kapyong is a sure-fire thriller. It has all the ingredients of a terrific saga, full of gunfire and danger, of heroism and sacrifice. It's also full of Canadians. It's the classic story of the few against the many.

An American Civil War general argued that battles aren't won by the generals, no matter how brilliant they are. A general's job is to get his soldiers to the battlefield. After that, it's all up to his men. Will they fight or not fight? Generals can lose battles, but to win battles, well, that's determined by the men. Jim Stone, the gruff, hawk-nosed commander who led the defence at Kapyong, agreed.

Long after the battle, twenty years later, he told a younger generation of Princess Patricia Canadian Light Infantry (PPCLI) officers the most important weapon in their arsenal was a factor that was almost spiritual, although such a hard man would never have used that soft phrase.

"There was something of much greater importance at Kapyong than the tactics of defence," he told his audience. "Kapyong demonstrated that morale, spirit of the troops, or call it what you will, is probably the most important factor in battle; and all the logistical support, the finest plans and the many other factors that are considered as requirements to fight a battle are subsidiary to it."[1]

The 2nd battalion of the Patricias went to Korea because they volunteered. They wanted to be there. At Kapyong, they had simply decided they could, despite the awful arithmetic, tough it out alone on their rocky hill and prevail.

It is an utter enigma why the Korean War, and the story within it of Kapyong and other valiant stands, has vanished from this country's memory. It's more than the Forgotten War: it's the war that never happened, scarcely touched on in high school history courses.

It is a fantasy to believe this country's military story is one of dedication to neutrality and peacekeeping. We have a long history as a people in arms. This country fought in the Boer War, sent a 6,000-man force to intervene in the Russian Civil War, and, of course, was a major player in the two greatest wars in history. Canada was one of the founding members of North Atlantic Treaty Organization (NATO), a military alliance specifically formed to be prepared for war with the Soviet Union. To back up our commitment to fight, we had hundreds of fighter aircraft and thousands of troops permanently stationed in Germany until the mid-1990s when the Cold War ended. Lester B. Pearson, who was a Nobel Peace Prize winner, was one of NATO's most passionate defenders and did not automatically reject force as an instrument of national policy. Canadians (in a pre-Confederation Canada) as individuals volunteered and fought in Cuba's war of Independence in the 1800s, and one man, Toronto-born William Ryan, was captured and executed by the Spanish. His portrait, flanked by a Canadian flag, is displayed at a memorial in Havana today where Ryan is an honoured hero in Castro's Cuba. Canadians in their tens of thousands fought in the American Civil War. In the Spanish Civil War no country aside from France had a greater proportion of its population involved. Canadians were with Castro in the hills fighting and running guns to his guerrillas. Other Canadians went to Rhodesia to fight guerrillas there. Many Canadians have fought for Israel in its many wars against the Arabs, and one of this country's most illustrious Spitfire pilots, Buzz Beurling, died in a mysterious crash while running arms to the fledgling Jewish state. About 30,000 Canadians volunteered to fight in Vietnam, including the son of a chief of the Canadian defence staff, who died there in the battle for Hue. Almost 120 Canadians have been killed in U.N. peacekeeping missions, including nine who died in a U.N. plane deliberately shot down by the Syrians in 1974. In Korea, fifty Canadians were killed in the two years after the armistice was signed.

It is simply untrue to believe this is a nation without a military tradition. And so it remains baffling why Korea, and Kapyong in particular, has been air-brushed out of our national story. Max Hastings, the British military historian, has suggested that if the Canadians at Kapyong had been massacred and no one had come down off the hill alive … well … that's the way to be remembered in history books. But that's the history that happily didn't happen.

Jack Granatstein, a prolific military historian and former head of the Canadian War Museum in Ottawa, has given much thought to the question: "Who killed Canadian history?" In a story so uncomplicated and easy to grasp and so full of heroes from central casting, why is Kapyong not the stuff of movies and TV dramas? Why aren't there parks and boulevards and high schools and scholarships named to commemorate this stirring tale of Canadian courage?

> It was a small war. It was sixty years ago. Those are the key factors right off the bat.
>
> Kapyong was a big battle for the battalion involved, but there were ten fatalities; a pretty small battle. It isn't D-Day; it isn't Falaise. Coming after the Second World War, where there were 5,000 fatalities at Normandy, it

was pretty small-scale. If it's been neglected there may be a reason. I think that's the key.

Korea was a sideshow in Canadian eyes even at the time. The country was going through a real burst of post-war prosperity, helped along by re-armament certainly, but Korea was a small war in a part of the world that Canadians didn't pay much attention to and had never done so in the past.[2]

Far away, perhaps, but it was a brutal, exhausting slogging match for those who were actually there on the snow-covered winter hills and in the boiling summers (the temperatures reached eighty degrees Fahrenheit at the time of Kapyong, and Canadian soldiers were still stuck with their heavy winter battle jackets). The casualties in Korea, where Canada had men in combat for only two years, were horrendous compared to Afghanistan, where Canadians have been fighting for almost a decade.

"Afghanistan matters more than Korea, if I can put it that way," says Granatstein. "It deals with something that is apparent in Western society: in other words, Islamisation, Islamist radicalism. It follows on 9/11. Korea didn't have anything like that to bring it home at the beginning. That shapes the way Afghanistan is seen and Korea is not."

The British have a knack of giving glorious life to their martial exploits, even to their fiascos. Churchill said of a particular defeat: "If this is a victory in disguise, it is very well disguised." The British learned about spin and public relations long before Madison Avenue got in on the act. Long ago the British mastered the trick of turning even a debacle into a triumph. At the same time that the Canadians were winning at Kapyong, the British Gloucestershire Regiment under the same kind of attack, a few miles to their west, was almost wiped out.

"The Glorious Glosters, the British battalion, it got creamed and yet got much more press than the PPCLI because it was creamed," says Granatstein. "Defeats go over better than victories, in a sense. Think of the way we wallow in Dieppe. It's a great defeat. 'We were betrayed.' 'The British did it to us.' We love defeats. Maybe it's because we expect victories. Defeats sink in more because they're unusual for us."

There is something strangely alluring about the martyrdom of glorious defeat, unless you were there in person, in the thick of it, on the losing side. Defeat can have a greater pull on the imagination and on patriotism than the hard-fought victory. Everyone remembers the Alamo. But no one remembers the battle of San Jacinto six weeks later when those same victors at the Alamo got trounced in a battle that was over in twenty minutes.

And it can't simply be the "smallness" of Kapyong that's relegated it to oblivion in Canadian history courses. Other countries manage to make a big deal of small battles. There were half as many Texans at the Alamo as at Kapyong. In the gallant British stand at Rorke's Drift in the Zulu War in southern Africa, made famous in the movie *Zulu* with Michael Caine, there were a quarter as many as at Kapyong. At the most-filmed, most written-about, most argued-over, least-consequential gunfight in history, the O.K. Corral, nine men shot it out, and it was all over in thirty seconds. Size doesn't count in the Famous Battle Sweepstakes.

So if "smallness" and "winning" cannot entirely account for the public ignorance of Kapyong, what remains to explain such indifference? Perhaps Canadians just feel uncomfortable and ill-at ease with heroes — our own heroes, at least.

David Bercuson, director of the Centre for Military and Strategic Studies at the University of Calgary, holds out little hope that the sixtieth anniversary of Kapyong and other Korean battles will rouse Canadian consciousness in the way the Steven Spielberg epic *Saving Private Ryan* rekindled the Second World War in the public imagination for a new generation.

Bercuson says it's always been a tough sell to generate excitement for a conflict that basically became a war of patrols, even when it was being fought.

"I was a young guy back then when it was on," says Bercuson. (He was five when it started.) "I remember listening to the radio: this hill or that hill had been attacked or not attacked. That's a kind of dull and boring war, not to the guys on the hill, certainly, but to folks here."[3]

"The war was on people's minds only at the beginning, at the very start," he says. "There was no real antiwar movement. People just soon became indifferent to it. It became the Forgotten War right in the middle of the war. At some point their interest just stopped."

On the sixtieth anniversary of the outbreak of the war, the *Globe and Mail* newspaper carried only two items marking the occasion: a column from Bercuson and a letter from the South Korean ambassador. That was it. No news story from anywhere. No editorial.

It's odd and speaks to the overwhelming disinterest in both the war and in Kapyong. Kapyong was strategically important. The Americans think so, as do the British and the Australians, too, who fought next to the Patricias on the neighbouring hill.

Britain and Australia both produced large and comprehensive official Korean War histories. Canada's official history of the Korea War is what Bercuson refers to as "this little book."

By the 1970s Canadian governments and schools were downplaying wars as a significant factor in Canadian history. At one point Canadian culture found the idea of Canadian heroes not to its taste. But not now, says Bercuson, Afghanistan has oddly changed that. Now we like our heroes.

"Opposition has grown to the war," he says, "but it's not the casualties: rather it's a combination of the casualties and no clear message. Canadians aren't sure what it's about any more. There's a growing feeling from the public that we're not going to win this thing no matter what we do."

But this has not translated into being wary of heroes. In fact, the public largely now has great admiration for Canada's soldiers.

"Canadians have changed. Afghanistan has changed people's views on the military and they understand what they're about and they accept it," says Bercuson.

But if admiration of soldiers and their patriotism had taken root, this had not translated into interest in what they were doing six decades ago in Asia. The sixtieth anniversary of Kapyong has slim hope of planting seeds of lasting renewed interest in Canada's Korean experience. A *Private Ryan* moment seems unlikely.

We've had about the same number of troops serve in Korea as have served in Afghanistan, but our population meantime has about doubled and our casualties are far fewer. So, proportionally, far fewer people are committed to the fight and fewer feel the pain. If Canadians have almost no memory of Korea and Kapyong, why in the years to come would they ever remember Afghanistan and Operations Anaconda and Medusa and Mountain Fury and all the others?

"When people think about veterans disappearing, Greatest Generation and all that," says Bercuson, "they don't really think about Korea. I'm sure we'll see the same thing happening to Afghanistan twenty years down the road."

Now-familiar names such as Kandahar or Panjwaii would then slowly become as obscure, dimly remembered, and then finally forgotten, as is Kapyong.

This is all a great pity. The Kapyong story sparkles with qualities that Canadians like to believe make up their national character: courage, initiative, modesty, and an uncomplicated, rock-solid belief in themselves.

This is not, hopefully, another war book. It is possible to tell this story without understanding military terms or unit structures, or caring what CMMFE, or BAR, or Chicom or CIC of U.N. Command or Operation Killer means; or where Kansas Line or Wyoming Line really are; or the difference between an F-86 and a P-80, between a colonel and a corporal; or how the Fifth Phase Offensive differed from the Fourth Phase Offensive; or that the DMZ keeps DPRK and ROK apart. None of this matters to tell this story. The people in this story are what matter. They are like those you pass on the street every day without giving them a moment's thought. But on one April night six decades ago, they were wonderful. So keep track of a handful of names that keep popping in and out of the narrative as it goes along, and you can easily follow Kapyong. It's a great tale.

The Canadians held on and won at Kapyong because they believed they were the best men on the hill that night. And they were right.

CHAPTER 1

CANADA IS NOT SIR GALAHAD

I f only they'd listened to Mackenzie King.

On a treacherous moonlit night, on a rocky, nowhere hill in Korea, desperate Canadian soldiers fought for their lives. April 24, 1951, was a night of great terror and much heroism.

Ken Barwise, a giant, six-foot lumber worker from Penticton, B.C., scrambled forward, dodging gunfire as he dashed to recover a captured machine gun and used it to blaze away in the darkness at the enemy soldiers that swarmed around him. Nearby, Smiley Douglas, a construction worker from tiny Elnora, Alberta, reached down in a frantic attempt to get rid of a live grenade that landed in the middle of his platoon. He was a micro-second too late.

Back home, you'd never know what Canada was up to over in Korea that night. As these events unfolded, that evening's edition of the Toronto *Globe and Mail* told its readers that Trans-Canada Airlines expected to show a profit. Con Smyth said that year's Maple Leafs were the best ever. Mink stoles were on sale for $1,200. Coca Cola cost a nickel.

And back in Korea that night, nineteen-year-old Wayne Mitchell from Vancouver was wounded in the eye as he was forced to abandon his trench. He fought on, blazing away with his submachine gun, and was almost overrun again as bodies piled up around him. Charging into the midst of the enemy, he took a second bullet, this time in the chest. It was also a desperate time for Mike Levy from Vancouver. As a teenager he'd fought as a guerrilla behind Japanese lines in Malaya. Now he was in his

Photo by Hub Gray.

Lieutenant Mike Levy, commanding officer of 10 Platoon, D Company, 2 PPCLI.

second Asian war, with his small, isolated platoon about to be swamped by hundreds of Chinese soldiers. In a last ditch attempt to save his men, Levy called in artillery fire on his own position. Just to the south of Levy, Hub Gray, who as a boy in Winnipeg had dreamed of joining the Navy, was light years away from sailing the seas. He spotted enemy soldiers in their hundreds manoeuvring in the darkness to attack the main command post from the rear. If it fell, so would the entire Canadian position, and then perhaps the whole front. Only Gray's men stood in the way. With the Chinese only a few meters away, he ordered his 50-calibre heavy machine gun crews to open up.

Meanwhile, the *Globe's* sports columnist in that night's edition warned that baseball was becoming big business. Someone dressed up like a doctor in an advertisement assured us that Buckingham cigarettes were "throat easy." And at Loews Uptown movie theatre, the hit *Abbot and Costello Meet the Invisible Man* was going into its second big week. Admission: 35 cents.

There was a single wire service story on page one about the war raging in Korea. "Reds Rip Gaping Hole in UN Line,"[1] shouted the headline. There was no mention anywhere that Canadian soldiers are in the thick of it.

They were, in fact, trapped on a place referred to as Hill 67' everyone on 677 called it simply Kapyong.

To many dug in on Kapyong, it certainly looked like their last night on earth. Don Hibbs, a taxi driver from Galt, Ontario, wanted only to escape from the dreary life of a cabbie. He joined the army just for the sheer adventure of fighting in Korea. It was shaping up as the worst decision of what was starting to look like his very short life. *We're never going to make it*, he thought. *There's just too many of them. This is where I'm going to die.*

How on earth did these young men — most scarcely out of high school, from farms and small towns, from lumber camps and construction crews, whose fathers, older brothers, and uncles had just finished crushing the Nazis — how did they ever end up on the edge of oblivion in the dead of night surrounded by thousands of Chinese peasants armed to the teeth in an unknown country? How did this happen? And how would they get out?

Canada had backed into the Korean story. If only someone had listened to Mackenzie King's warnings. King's instincts had been dead on from the start: steer clear of Korea.

Domestic tranquility, not the messy world of foreign policy, was his comfort zone. The lonely, mystic prime minister had a keen instinct of how human nature functioned and how seemingly simple matters could quickly be made to unravel into a nightmare by well-meaning busybodies. Daring, flamboyant gestures were dangerous and not to his political taste. To this master politician, Korea just didn't feel right.

In late 1947, the United Nations wanted Canada to help supervise elections in Korea, newly liberated from Japan and jointly occupied by the Americans and the Soviets.

King had a superb sense of what worked and what didn't. And Korea, his senses told him, was something that didn't. He confided these broodings to his diary and maybe to his best (and perhaps only) friend and confident — his dog Pat.

King knew nothing about Korea and that stark fact told him all he needed to know about how to proceed, or not to proceed. King could smell trouble.

"Canada's role was not that of Sir Galahad to save the world,"[2] he wrote in his now-famous diary.

To his fury, King, in December 1947, discovered that his external affairs minister, Louis St. Laurent, and his representative at the United Nations, Lester Pearson (both future prime ministers), had volunteered Canada's participation in the election commission.

King liked none of this. It was all just too dreamy. And too far away. He confided to his diary: "… a great mistake was being made by Canada being brought into situations of which she knew nothing whatever … without realizing what the consequences might be."

Picking up steam as he wrote, King roasted Pearson for his "youth and experience," implying his man at the U.N. was a little full of himself in offering up Canada for service in Korea before either he or the cabinet had thought it all through.

There were no Canadian interests at stake in Korea. We had no historic, commercial, or cultural ties with the place. The only Canadians over there were a handful of missionaries and a few mining engineers.

Fighting the Nazis and the Japanese empire in the greatest war in history, which had ended only two years earlier, was one thing. That was strategic and vital. But Korea was a land of utter mystery and misery and utterly unimportant to anyone, except Koreans. There was, he wrote, no one in the cabinet who knew anything at all about the place. What started out as helping to supervise a simple election could quietly and quickly morph into something lethal and dangerous. King, with remarkable insight for a politician with a modest world view, sensed that involvement in Korea involved unforeseen, messy repercussions and could someday, in some way — he wasn't sure how — draw Canada into a war in Asia. As it turned out, the unification elections for Canada to help supervise were never held — and Korea to this day is famously un-unified — but the seeds of Canada's Korean involvement that so worried King were germinating. King had been right; no one had ever heard of the place. But the clock had now begun ticking in the countdown on Canada's road to Kapyong.

CHAPTER 2

JACK JAMES'S SCOOP

Korea is in a tough neighbourhood, and has been seen as fair game by its rapacious neighbours.

Korea is a strange country that for centuries has had most of the prerequisites for nationhood, including a distinct language and culture. And for more than 700 years it's been on someone's invasion list: first the Mongols came, and then the Chinese. Most recently the Japanese outright occupied the country in the early 1900s and savagely suppressed all Korean dissent. Despite all this, the Koreans have retained a sense of their Koreanness. They never viewed their rule by foreigners as anything other than illegal. And temporary.

With the surrender of Japan in September 1945, the Soviets and the Americans moved in to jointly occupy and administer the country, dividing it at the 38th parallel. After all that was to happen in the bloody years ahead, it's roughly that same border that divides the country to this day. The Cold War set in. U.N. election observer ring teams, with Canada on board, were not allowed into the north. Instead, the Soviets set up and armed a brutal Stalinist regime, leaving their strongman, Kim Il-Sung, in charge. In the south, where elections were held, a pro-western strongman, Harvard and Princeton graduate Syngman Rhee, got the most seats in parliament (but not a majority) and became president. Both were tough and ruthless men, and both claimed to speak for one Korea.

There followed a period of low-intensity violence between the two hostile Koreas: raids, ambushes, shellings, snipings, and kidnappings. But nothing got out of hand.

Then, around eight o'clock on a sleepy Sunday morning on June 25, 1950, Jack James, a well-connected correspondent for the United Press wire agency walked into the American embassy in Seoul with the scoop of a lifetime.

"The North Koreans have crossed over the parallel in force!" he announced to a marine guard on duty.

The bored duty sergeant said simply, "So what? This is a common occurrence."

"Yeah," said James. "But this time they've got tanks."[1]

Jack James's exclusive beat the State Department announcement by two hours. The Korean War was on.

It was almost a very short campaign. The tough, well-trained, and well-equipped North Koreans swept aside the South Koreans and the capital was evacuated. American occupation forces based in Japan were sent to try to salvage the unfolding disaster.

The U.N. Security Council, boycotted at the time by the U.S.S.R., voted to come to South Korea's defence with uncharacteristic speed. This decision would eventually lead to an international fighting force from almost twenty countries, lead by the U.S. and fighting under a U.N. banner. "Neutralist" countries such as Sweden and India sent medical teams. Even tiny Luxembourg, a member of the newly-founded NATO, sent forty-four soldiers.

In Ottawa, however, there was great hesitation. Even the defence minister was wary of getting involved with what he feared would become some endless American adventure in Asia. But Lester Pearson was among those saying it would be very difficult to say "No" to the Americans if they insisted Canada join in sending combat troops to Korea to drive back a blatant example of communist aggression.

Eventually Canada did climb board. In August, Prime Minister Louis St. Laurent (external affairs minister under Mackenzie King, who had only died a few weeks earlier and whose ghost must have been uneasy at what was about to be announced) declared that Canadians would be going to Korea to fight. Canada was a driving force in the founding of the new North Atlantic Treaty Organization and was being governed by a generation of Atlantic-minded men. Europe's defence against the Soviets was their obsession.

There was also little taste for another Canadian military venture in Asia after the disaster at Hong Kong in the last war, in which ill-trained and badly led troops had been sacrificed for no apparent reason and were captured and brutally treated (and often murdered) by the Japanese. Canada's sacrifice in the Hong Kong debacle seemed, to many, to be serving mainly Britain's interests. And now there was a similar unease that the war revving up in Korea was to serve Washington's agenda more than Canada's or the U.N.'s. But other countries were not hesitating to contribute combat forces, including fellow Commonwealth cousins such as Britain and Australia. So, too, were fellow NATO allies, such as Turkey and Greece, which couldn't possibly be any further away from Korea. And the Americans, with Munich ever on their minds, felt this was a classic case of a testing of resolve in standing up against clear-cut aggression.

Munich symbolized the meek capitulation of Britain and France to Hitler's demands to take over Czechoslovakia, making the Second World War a virtual certainty. Munich forever gave "appeasement" a bad name. The Munich ghost made several return visits to American foreign policy in the years ahead, providing some of the philosophic and moral unpinning in justifying intervention in Vietnam a decade after Korea, and the toppling of Saddam Hussein a half century into the future. Munich has had a long shelf life. Korea would not be abandoned as Czechoslovakia had been. If a Korea-style U.N. force had been available to defend the Czechs in the late 1930s, the thinking went, Hitler's invasion schemes could have been stopped cold.

The international U.N. force being put together was quite unlike anything that followed. It was not a peace-observing mission, or even peace-keeping. There was no peace to keep. It was a fighting force heading, by design, straight into harm's way.

It was truly a "coalition of the willing," in some cases with traditional foes such as Greece and Turkey fighting on the same side. All were more-or-less democracies. All would pay a heavy price in blood, including countries such as Columbia, with 146 killed, and Turkey with over 800 killed. (The group cohesion of the Turks was so strong that their captured soldiers had the highest survival rate in the brutal Chinese POW camps.) Ethiopia sent what it called "Conqueror Battalions" and had 122 killed. Thailand had 136 killed; Belgium, 97; Greece, 190; and tiny Luxembourg had seven killed.

Italy, which was not a U.N. member at the time (it had actually been an enemy country and fought at Hitler's side in the war which ended only six years earlier), sent a Red Cross unit.

Norway and Denmark each sent a hospital ship. Sweden sent a field hospital, which stayed on long after the war ended. India sent a MASH unit, which was much praised by the Canadian wounded, and also sent a medical team that accompanied American paratroopers when they jumped into combat.

Many countries, Canada included, won U.S. Presidential Citations from President Truman for feats of particular bravery. Two British units received such citations, as did one from Australia (at Kapyong); also Belgium, Turkey, Greece, France, a South African Air Force Squadron, and Holland, whose Regiment Van Heutsz, received the citation twice.

Korea was a remarkable example of shared international sacrifice and reflected a highly diverse array of religions and cultures that held intact throughout the entire conflict. No one dropped out along the way. Canada, after a confused start, was to be in to the finish.

On August 7, about six weeks after the invasion, Prime Minister St. Laurent announced that a "special force" would be raised specifically to go into combat to help defend the embattled South Koreans. The march to Kapyong had started.

This would not be a war, St. Laurent stressed, not a "real war" at any rate, but a "police action." And it would not be an American war, he emphasized. Rather, it would be run under the United Nations flag. This was a quaint legal nicety. The Americans provided the leadership, in large part American equipment and weapons would be used, and Americans were providing, by far, most of the troops. And, most importantly, the U.S. military was certainly charting the war's overall direction and strategy. Aside from the Koreans themselves, the Americans were doing most of the fighting and most of the dying, so the war would be run their way. When Truman once suggested he would not rule out the use of nuclear weapons in Korea, a startled British Prime Minister Clement Attlee quickly flew to Washington for assurances Britain would be consulted first. He was given no such assurances. There was no doubt: as the senior partner, the U.S. was calling the shots in this war, although as we shall see when the Americans tried to rush Canadian troops into combat prematurely, their commander bravely, and successfully, stood up to U.S. bullying.

St. Laurent's phrase "police action" never sat well with the troops who were doing the shooting and dying, and was seen as outright hypocrisy intended to lull the folks back home into thinking nothing too serious was happening. An additional problem was that, technically, if no actual war was declared, then where was the process that would someday end it? How do you undeclare a war that was never declared? And in a dilemma that Canada and its allies in Afghanistan would face decades later, what exactly was victory anyway; what exactly would "winning" look like? Was winning simply driving the invaders out of South Korea? Or was it to crush the North Korean Army? Or was it, more ominously, to destroy the North Korean state? The war aims changed and morphed as the war dragged on, and many of the more drastic end-scenarios were mused about rather than stated. Everyone, it seemed, had their own definition about what the point of it all was, where it was leading, and how it would wrap up.

This was a fuzzy, new world that the military felt quite uncomfortable in. The Americans were not at all at ease the idea of fighting for anything less than total victory. In this reality, they were not out to destroy North Korea as Japan and Nazi Germany had been crushed. They were merely there to stop North Korea's aggression, which meant American pilots were forbidden to even fly into Chinese airspace in pursuit of Chinese jet-fighter aircraft (sometimes secretly flown by Soviet pilots) fleeing back into their safe havens once China stepped in. Fighting a limited war was so contrary to American military doctrine and culture that it created a profound crisis in which the President Harry Truman fired his popular (with the public at least, if not in the Pentagon) war commander, Douglas MacArthur, who threw out broad hints of invading China. The frustration of fighting to win something less than "victory" didn't seem to bedevil Canada's soldiers, who just lived with it, but it infuriated America's military. As it turned out, fighting would finally end, not with surrender or a peace treaty, but with an armistice, which was a military, not a political document. That armistice is still in effect today and in a technical sense the "war" is still on, it's just on hold. But among all soldiers on the sharp end of events, out in the hills, the "police action" phrase would later take on an acidic taste as Korea turned into a meat grinder.

Ted Zuber, a war artist, reflected on the bitterness on being told he wasn't in a "real" war. "I can remember some people saying, 'Well, that's not like the Second World War.' And I said tell that to the guy that got wounded or died over there. A bullet couldn't give a goddamn what war it is," Ted Zuber told the author many years ago.

Zuber was not at Kapyong, but served as a sniper later in the war and was wounded. After Korea he became a distinguished painter and combat artist and many of his paintings are in the Canada War Museum in Ottawa. The Zuber painting on the cover of this book depicts a night patrol in Korea. A Chinese flare shoots up, catching the Canadian squad exposed and helpless in no man's land. The men "freeze," fearful that any movement would give them away to Zuber's counterparts, the Chinese snipers lying in ambush. Zuber was a combat infantryman of great experience and several of his works depict the fight at Kapyong. He was Canada's official war artist in the First Gulf War of 1991.

Yard for yard, bomb for bomb, bullet for bullet, hour for hour, Korea was as relentless a killing factory as any "real" war. To an infantry soldier it was every bit as violent and deadly as the Second World War. In many ways it resembled, especially in its latter stages, the stalemated but treacherous trench warfare of the First World War. It was such a bloodbath that it is so odd that it is so little remembered or written about today. More than 36,000 Americans were killed in Korea, as were more than 500 Canadians. China may have lost 1.5 million; no one knows. And all this in just three years. This war in Korea is now strangely vanished, but it was a remorseless slogging match and all soldiers who fought there, including Canadians, to this day deeply resent the absurd "police action" description, a seemingly ridiculous label, they say, dreamed up by international law specialists and diplomats sitting safely back home, not by the people doing the fighting.

Canada entered this war wondering where on earth it would find the soldiers to fight it. After cutbacks at the end of the Second World War, in Canada the army alone had been slashed from 700,000 down to 16,000.

To maintain new NATO commitments in Europe, which were aimed at meeting a very grave and immediate concern, namely defending Europe against the U.S.S.R., Canada's new Korean fighting formations had to come from somewhere new; some, as yet, untapped resource. A new fighting force was to be created from scratch, not from the existing army.

Canada's special Korean force would be formed into a new brigade of around 5,000 men. Three new battalions would be grafted onto regular army existing regiments. For example, the Princess Patricia's Canadian Light Infantry already had one battalion and the new one would be designated the 2nd. And it was this new force, 2 PPCLI as it was termed (and still is today), that would be the first to go into combat in Korea, and would become the most famous fighting unit in the Canadian army since the Second World War.

Princess Patricia's Canadian Light Infantry: an odd sort of name. A military force that describes itself using the words "Princess," "Patricia," and "Light" doesn't sound as if it's serious about its work. But from its inception, PPCLI staked out a reputation as being tenacious and rock-solid reliable.

The "Light" part of the name implies they were fast moving and mobile, relying on stealth and fitness; light as in "travel light." They are often regarded as elite units. Commandos, mountain troops, marines, and anti-guerrilla forces are regarded as "light." Historically, they were snipers and skirmishers. Medium and heavy infantry usually dates to a pre-gunpowder era and refers to the use body armour, javelins, and pikes. Most infantry in modern armies, whatever their names, are light infantry.

But who is Patricia, and what was she doing in Korea?

The PPCLI is one of the most decorated forces in Canadian history. It was created when the First World War broke out in the very twilight of the Victorian age. Canada's entire regular army was only 3,000-men strong. It was a time when private individuals — rich private individuals — could actually create their own military units, and, not unlike medieval times, put them at the service of the nation. These philanthropists would often provide the rifles, the clothing, and the upkeep. Sometimes they designed their own uniforms, and on occasion even thought, *well, it's mine. Why don't I command it?*

Montreal businessman and Boer War veteran Alexander Hamilton Gault had a brainstorm. He would personally come up with $100,000 (about $2 million in today's funds) to raise a battalion to go and fight the Germans as part of Canada's contribution to beating the Kaiser. Ottawa snapped up the offer, and in eight days over 1,000 men were enlisted, little dreaming what a bloodbath they were heading into. Lieutenant Colonel Francis D. Farquhar of the Coldstream Guards was selected to command the new force. His boss happened to be the Governor General, the Duke of Connaught, who just happened to have a lovely daughter, Patricia, who was a granddaughter of Queen Victoria and an accomplished artist who lived on until 1974. Farquhar's flash of insight was to ask the Duke if he could name the regiment after Patricia.

Gault liked the words "light infantry" because it had an "irregular" sort of commando feel to it. And so, "Princess Patricia's Canadian Light Infantry" it became. And still is.

The Patricias were in the trenches of Flanders by January 6, 1915. Two days later, two lance corporals, Norman Fry and Henry Bellinger, were dead — the first Canadians killed in the War to End All Wars. They would be joined by thousands more. By the time the shooting stopped, three Patricias had won the Victoria Cross, two posthumously. Almost 1,300 men had been killed.

The Patricias' "colours" suggest they were sent to Siberia. It is listed on their official list of where they saw action. But actually, they never got into Siberia. In 1918, Canada sent a small contingent of about 1,000 men in an outfit called the 260th Battalion to Vladivostok as part of a half-hearted foreign intervention in the Russian Civil War. The men of the 260th never fired a shot in anger and in a few weeks were brought home. Fast forward eighty years. In 1997, in a quirky and uniquely Canadian system that insures the deeds of disbanded combat units are remembered, the PPCLI agreed to safeguard and in effect adopt the 260th's "heritage" and now carries that long defunct battalion's Siberian battle honour, even though no Patricia ever set foot in the place.

In the Second World War, the PPCLI fought in Sicily for the first Canadian assault on the Nazis since the debacle at Dieppe. Then they moved on to the Italian mainland and a grueling string of battles against crack German troops in wretched weather and treacherous terrain.

Then they headed over to Holland for the Liberation and by the time of Germany's surrender the battalion had acquired eighteen battle honours. They were headed for the Pacific to take on Japan when Hiroshima and Nagasaki ended the war. They had a magnificent war record and a reputation as tough, imaginative troops.

But these existing Patricias were, by and large, not the Patricias that would go to Korea. The Korean force would come from those three new battalions the army would create from nothing. The first to go to war, the men fated to become the Patricias of Kapyong, formed the 2nd Battalion of Princess Patricia's Canadian Light Infantry, or 2 PPCLI as its termed in military shorthand. These new Patricias were joining a family with a fine and noble lineage. It was a distinction that probably meant little to these recruits who were mostly young, mostly restless, on the prowl for excitement, and who were sneeringly dismissed by the brass in Ottawa as untrustworthy adventurers whose favorite marching song contained the line they shouted with pride: "We're untrained bums, we're from the slums."

In command of the three battalions of the Korean Special Force was John Rockingham, a Second World War veteran brought out of retirement for this special mission. He looked, sounded, and acted exactly like what everyone imagined a magnetic commander would be like. He was a Gibraltar of a figure who literally towered over everyone around him. Rockingham was a dashing, charismatic leader right out of a recruiting poster, who led from the front. He joined the militia as a private and ended his career as a general, commanding the 9th Canadian Infantry brigade in Europe. He led his men through some of the bloodiest fighting in the war, eastward across France and Holland, and on into Germany. In one action, his driver and signaller beside him were shot by a sniper and Rockingham's own nose was clipped by a bullet. He grabbed a submachine gun, stalked the sniper, shot him, and then resumed the war. He was slated to command a brigade of Canadian troops to fight the Japanese, when Hiroshima happened and the Pacific War ended.

Rockingham's soldiers felt he was one of them and would follow wherever he led. He was a restless warrior and had no interest in being in the military at all unless there was fighting to be done. Rockingham was an improviser with the ability to rivet his attention on the crisis at hand

PPCLI Museum and Archives.

Brigadier General John "Rocky" Rockingham, a much-decorated Second World War hero, was plucked from his tedious job as union negotiator for a B.C. bus company to command the special Canadian force being created to fight in Korea. It was an inspired choice. Rockingham was a fighting general who had no interest in a life in the army unless there was fighting to be done.

and not be distracted by peripheral matters; an ideal commander to take charge in Korea.

In August 1950, he had an unbearably boring desk job with a British Columbia bus company. He was in charge of tedious union contract negotiations. To this real-life action figure used to making instant life and death decisions involving of thousands of men, his biggest issue now was over the issue of lunch breaks. The give and take and compromise so much at the heart of negotiating was not to his nature. He was a commander. Then, happily, in the midst of deadlocked contract talks, his phone rang. It was Ottawa on the line. It was a life-changing call for Rockingham. They were offering him command of the Korean special force and he could pick his own staff. Rockingham checked with his wife and the next day accepted. Two days later he was in Ottawa starting to organize his Korean army. He was only thirty-nine. He was rightly perceived as a seasoned combat leader who was coming not from the military culture but from civilian life. He would protect Canadian interests while serving under a foreign (American) command and would stick up for his men. In particular, he would work well with the Americans on a personal level and there could be no doubting his professional credentials, although once he got to Korea Rockingham would often clash with his U.S. officers over their emphasis on body counts as a measure of progress, a questionable yardstick which would afflict the U.S. military fifteen years later in Vietnam. Rockingham was a charismatic bulldog of a man. He was an inspired choice, and was selected personally by the minister of defence, Brooke Claxton.

One of Rockingham's choices was Lieutenant-Colonel "Big Jim" Stone, one of the most talented and innovative soldiers in Canadian history.

He looked like something from a Marx Brothers movie, sporting a huge walrus moustache that made him resemble a puffed-up, desk-bound, self-important, Colonel Blimp-type figure from *Punch* magazine. He was none of those things. Kapyong is impossible to understand without understanding Jim Stone.

In 1939 he was working in a forestry camp in northern Alberta. When war broke out in September he was thirty-one, an absurdly ancient age to start an army career. He mounted his horse, Minnie, rode her 30 miles to Spirit River, then thumbed a ride to Grand Prairie, and enlisted as a private in the Edmonton Regiment. His aura of natural leadership and toughness were quickly spotted and he was promoted through the ranks and fast-tracked into officer's training.

Brigadier General John Rockingham (centre, with Scottish headwear) and Colonel Jim Stone (right of Rockingham, with moustache).

Stone fought first in Italy, in Canada's first battles with the Nazis since the debacle at Dieppe the year before. Italy was a tough, mountainous, wild place to fight an infantry war against crack German troops. Stone was at the centre of the bitter house-to-house battles around Ortona, where he established a reputation as an aggressive commander of great tactical skill — a reputation enhanced by the precious care he took with the lives of his men.

In a typical Stone exploit, during fighting through rubble-strewn streets of Ortona, he wanted tanks to blast their way through an obstacle, helping pave the way for his infantry. In his classic account of the dreadful agony at Ortona, Mark Zuehlke captures the spirit of Jim Stone at his most cantankerous and his best:

> But suddenly, little more than 25 yards short of the rubble pile, the lead tank paused. The other tanks ground

to a halt, maintaining their preset intervals between each other. They also ceased firing their guns. The infantry milled, unsure what was happening. By pausing, the tankers were hopelessly messing up the attack. As an infantryman, Stone believed, it was an all-too-common experience. Stone jumped up on the lead tank. "What the hell's the matter?" he yelled. The tank commander pointed at a scrap of sheet metal lying in the road. "It's probably concealing a mine," he said. Stone was incredulous. The entire street, from one end to the other, was littered with bricks, stones, chunks of metal, broken boxes, and other debris from the battered and destroyed buildings fronting it. What made this piece of metal special? Stone tried to convince the man to get going again. He could feel the attack's momentum slipping through his fingers, like so many grains of wheat. The tank commander said petulantly, "Don't you realize a tank is worth $20,000? I can't risk it." "You armoured sissy," Stone snapped. "I've got 20 to 30 men here with no damned armour at all and they're worth a million dollars apiece."[2]

The attack bogged down. A German anti-tank gun started firing at the Canadian tanks. Stone yelled at his own anti-tank man to open fire with his PIAT, a British version of the bazooka. The man fired and missed and then began trying to reload. Stone had run out of patience. He tossed a smoke grenade at the German gun, then, all alone, began running towards it, pulling out a fragmentation grenade as he went, and tossed it over the gun's steel shield protecting the Germans, wiping them all out. He was awarded the Military Cross for his amazing day's work.

Stone was light years removed from military behind-the-lines, "chateau" commanders who gave their orders far removed from the front, inhabiting a different universe from the men they commanded. Stone lived, ate, and slept where his men did and took the same risks. And they knew it.

By war's end he'd become a lieutenant-colonel and gone on to fight his way into Germany. In addition to his Military Cross, he had been decorated with the Distinguished Service Order — twice.

One of his citations reads: "There were many instances (in Italy and Holland) where Lt-Col. Stone's personal leadership was the contributing factor to the success in battle. His initiative and courage are unsurpassed."

In Korea, he would drop in on his front line troops, and often walk along the crest of a hill offering himself as a live target, daring the Chinese to fire at him, which they did without result. It was Stone's way of telling his soldiers they were all in it together. Stone was Rockingham's personal choice to command 2 PPCLI, the first Canadian unit to go into combat in Korea.

Oddly, though decorated four times for bravery by the time he retired, in Korea Stone told his men that he didn't believe much in medals, so don't expect any.

The mountain warfare skills he mastered in the Italian campaign gave him precisely the insights that would be priceless later on at Kapyong. However, there was an important difference: in Italy he was attacking, where at Kapyong he'd be defending. But thanks to his Italian battles, he developed the vital knack of seeing things from the enemy's point of view.

Even in the decades that followed Korea, the men who fought in Stone's army had a strange attachment to the man. At a fiftieth anniversary ceremony in Kapyong itself, veterans made arrangements to phone Stone who could not attend because of poor health. When the call was made, a military bureaucrat from the Canadian embassy tried to break in and stop it because, he said, there was a ceremony taking place. He was curtly told by the veterans that they were making the call to the man who'd made the ceremony possible.

Jim Stone was a tough man to love and an easy one to admire. Some of his men asked specifically to serve under him. He was a special soldier, exactly the type of inspired and inspiring leader you'd want in a desperate situation. He was a popular choice; a fighting infantry commander who led from the front. A soldiers' soldier. The troops respected him, the press lionized him, and the public ate it up. A *Winnipeg Free Press* headline caught the tone exactly: "Big Jim From Ortona Rejoins The Army; Canada's 'Legend' To Head Unit In Korea."[3]

There was no shortage of volunteers for the special force. Ten days into the recruitment campaign 7,000 men had signed up. Their makeup was different than those who'd gone to war against Hitler only a few years earlier. That had been a crusade against an enormous evil, and virtually the entire nation rose up and joined in the struggle.

The volunteers for Korea were not by-and-large from the mainstream middle class, who were busy building comfortable careers and raising families in Canada's post-war prosperity. Korean volunteers, the enlisted men at least, were more likely to be working class. Officers and senior non-commissioned officers, such as sergeants, were likely to be veterans of the Second World War. But the private soldiers were mostly straight out of civilian life, with many still in their teens. This would be a citizen's army. These recruits joined up not just to be in the army, but to be in the army to fight, and to fight specifically in Korea. They were after adventure, certainly, but also because they wanted combat. There'd never been a Canadian military force quite like this before. These young men had not the least interest in the grand issues of politics or balance of power or ideology or any great moral crusade.

This was the army Stone wanted. He didn't want dreamers. He wanted fighters.

The Kapyong army was "recruited from the streets,"[4] as he once tersely put it in his talk to the new generation of PPCLI officers years later.

> Among them were many dead-beats, escapists from domestic troubles, cripples, neurotics and other useless types all of whom broke down under the rigorous training program and we got rid of them prior to going into action.
>
> Those who joined to fight for a cause were difficult to find. Bill Boss, our accompanying war correspondent, tried to find the idealist who joined solely to fight a holy war against Communism, like Diogenes searching with his lantern trying to find an honest man. Bill was unsuccessful.
>
> The strength of the Battalion was its adventurers, those who joined the army because there was a war to fight and they wanted to be there. Personally I believe that all volunteer armies in wartime are composed mostly of adventurers.[5]

Pierre Berton, the journalist, quickly spotted the absence of moral commitment in the Canadian troops, and he disapproved: "What struck me during my first few days with the Canadian troops," Berton wrote years later in *Maclean's* magazine, "was the appalling lack of understanding among the rank and file, who, for the most part, had no real idea why they were in Korea. They were tough, resourceful and skilled; they had exchanged shots with the enemy, and discipline was not a problem. But the Why We Fight kind of lecture that had been part of basic infantry training in the Global War wasn't part of the syllabus."[6]

Berton did not grasp that these men were a new, existential breed of soldier. They needed no pep talks or motivational lectures. They knew precisely why they had gone to war: they wanted to fight.

Don Hibbs, the twenty-year-old cab driver from Guelph, Ontario, asked himself: *What am I doing here in this stupid car when I could be in the army?*[7]

He'd missed the last war and he didn't want to miss this one.

"I can be a hero over there pulling hand grenades out with my teeth, was my impression. I joined basically for the adventure, not patriotism. I didn't even know where Korea was. I didn't care where Korea was. I just thought: I want to go to war. I want that experience."

John Bishop was working in British Columbia logging camps. He was nineteen and he, too, joined for the action. Some, he said, enlisted looking for adventure, but some simply "wanted to get away from wives. Or they were not in a good relationship with the police. I knew of only one man went over to fight communism. We joined to fight. We knew we were going to a fight. We were pretty proud. Almost all of us got out at the end of our [eighteen-month] tour. Very few became regulars."[8]

One of the few was Bishop, who went on to become a career soldier and diplomat, and later in life was posted to a peacetime Korea as military attaché at the Canadian embassy.

Another who simply liked the military life was Alex Sim of Kamloops, British Columbia. He was a Second World War veteran, who left the army after the war and then re-enlisted for Korea.

He felt and still feels it was the right thing to do.

"We had an obligation to go,"[9] he explains today. "The Koreans were taking a terrible beating. The Brits were going. The Aussies were going.

What's matter with Canada? We should be going. I wrote letter to someone in the government saying I was very disappointed Canada not going to assist. I never got an answer."

Sim had also a brother and a cousin in the same platoon. His cousin was given a medical evacuation because of an ear infection only a few days before Kapyong and so missed the battle.

"We never talk about it," says Sim.

To join up, recruits often showed great inventiveness. In Rivers, Manitoba, Mike Czuboka, fresh out of high school, hitched a ride on a freight train to Winnipeg to enlist, and then lied to the army about his age, claiming he was nineteen, not eighteen.

"According to official army records, I'm still that one year older than I really am,"[10] he says today.

Czuboka had felt he was missing out on a thrilling opportunity; something that would never come again. He worshiped his older brother who'd been in the RCAF and had flown fifty-two missions over the Atlantic hunting U-boats.

"I was fourteen years old when World War Two ended and I saw Korea as a chance for a great adventure of the kind I'd been denied in the War."

But he also had a sadder motive. His Ukrainian-born father was imprisoned during the First World War as an enemy alien and afterwards always felt he was an unwanted foreigner in his adopted country. Deeply hurt, young Mike Czuboka signed on for Korea in part "to prove [he] was a good Canadian."

But the excitement of combat was always a huge attraction to a young, restless prairie boy.

"If you want to be a soldier then combat is something you're looking forward to," says Czuboka. "It's the making of you. Specifically I went into the infantry because that's where the action is. There's no point in telling an infantryman it's a dangerous business; of course it's dangerous. It's like telling a race car driver they shouldn't race because it's dangerous. That's why they race."

In Mike Czuboka's mortar platoon the casualty rate was to be almost 30 percent.

Free spirits the volunteers may have been, but they were hardly the "soldiers of fortune" that the chief of the general staff, General Charles

Foulkes, labelled them. Curiously, it was an important civilian, the defence minister, Bruce Claxton, who was most impressed with the calibre of the recruits he'd met. But the military brass were always uneasy with the Korean special force, feeling, strangely, that people who actually wanted to fight a war were not the types wanted in the army. As it turned out, these were precisely the type of people who fought superbly.

Despite Foulkes' demeaning sneer, these young men turned out to be deadly serious. They were quick learners and imaginative improvisers, capable of great heroism. They seemed to be natural fighters with an uncanny ability to adapt to circumstances and make do with the resources at hand. These talents later turned out to be a great asset when they were sent into the fight with the wrong training and the wrong weapons for this odd war.

Such was the enthusiasm to enlist, an assortment of misfits and oddballs got in line. One man with an artificial leg managed to slip through the initial recruit medical examination. Another was seventy-two years old. In another instance a civilian, on a last-minute impulse, jumped on a troop train heading out of Ottawa and it was weeks later before he was finally discovered, drilling with PPCLI recruits way out in Alberta.

The three-battalion Korean force was eventually organized into a formation called the 25th Canadian Infantry Brigade and was to be concentrated in one place. Fort Lewis, near Tacoma, Washington was chosen. Training could be completed there and it was also closest to an embarkation port to the Far East.

The Fort Lewis venture had its tragic moment in late November.

One of the last trains bringing the troops out, at a hamlet called Canoe River, British Columbia, was winding its way westward through the Rockies and smashed head-on into an oncoming express as both were rounding the same curve. Seventeen men were killed. Four bodies were never found. Seventy were injured, many scalded, for these were the final days of the era of steam locomotives. Both the prosecution and the railway tried to pin the blame for the disaster on a lowly CNR telegrapher. The man was acquitted thanks to the flaming oratory and the brilliant defence presented by his lawyer, the underdog's ferocious champion and a man on his way up: a young Prairie firebrand named John Diefenbaker.

Back at the war, events had taken a dramatic new turn. It appeared to be winding down.

After an initial dismal showing, the Americans eventually held the line against the North Koreans. General Douglas MacArthur was put in charge and staged a brilliantly executed invasion in September on Korea's west coast at Inchon, quickly driving the North Koreans out of the south. MacArthur, who was steeped in military history, while planning the Inchon landing was reading James Wolfe's diaries about planning his fight against Montcalm at Quebec City. All of Wolfe's officers said Wolfe's plans were impossible and Wolfe decided if they thought so, then so would the French. Similarly, MacArthur reasoned if many of his own staff thought Inchon a dangerously unworkable idea, then so would the North Koreans. Inchon turned out to be MacArthur's masterpiece. The Americans were soon pushing on up the peninsula, seemingly unstoppable and heading ominously close to the Chinese border.

It now looked as if the North Korean army was finished as a fighting force and North Korea itself would soon be finished as a state. The war was all but over.

As it was shaping up, there now would be no need for all those fighting Canadians. What was now needed was not a combat force, but an occupation army.

With the pressure off, Canada decided to send only one unit of the three that had been formed: the 2nd Battalion of the Princess Patricia's Canadian Light Infantry. It would be made up of about 900 men. The great adventure now seemed destined to be something far less. Occupation duty offered no danger, certainly, but also no excitement. Danger and excitement were supposed to be part of the deal. To these young Canadian soldiers, it was the whole point.

An aging American Second World War-era troop ship named the USS *Private Joe P. Martinez* would take the Patricias from Seattle to Pusan, Korea. A U.S. Navy band saw them off, playing with great geographic if not musical accuracy, "It's a Long Way to Tipperary." The voyage was a nightmare and would last almost three agonizing weeks.

The poor old *Martinez* was a liberty ship. Cheap and churned out in their thousands, they were mass-produced to a single design to get quickly across the Atlantic to beat the U-Boats waiting in ambush. They took just a little over a month to build; although one was completed in four days as a publicity stunt. They were a masterpiece of American industrial assembly-line efficiency. About 2,500 were still in service at the end of the Second World War when hundreds were bought up by Greek shipping magnates, such as Aristotle Onassis, and formed the basis of their new empire of cargo fleets. Liberty ships were designed with one single aim in mind: they were no-frills workhorses. What they were not were passenger liners. Onto this wheezing, geriatric rust bucket were loaded almost 2,000 Canadian and American troops and all their paraphernalia of war.

The *Martinez* was named to honour a real-life hero, an American soldier, Joseph Martinez from Taos, New Mexico, who deserved a better memorial. The son of dirt-poor farm workers, he was the first Hispanic-American to be awarded the Medal of Honor. Although only a private, he personally led repeated attacks over snow-covered mountains against Japanese positions in the Aleutian Islands campaign, off the coast of Alaska. The Aleutian Campaign was an obscure theatre, little studied by historians and the only part of the Second World War fought on North American soil. It was a war fought in extreme weather, and rough terrain in a place hardly anyone involved in had ever heard of. It was remarkably like Korea.

But remote and neglected by history as the campaign is, men still died there. Joe Martinez was one of them. As he stormed the last Japanese trench on the island of Attu, Martinez was shot in the head and died the next day. Several army facilities and legion posts in the American southwest are today still named in his honour. Canadians in the elite Canadian-American Devil's Brigade also fought in the Aleutians. The exploits of this dashing, unconventional unit was the basis of the popular Hollywood movie starring William Holden. Part of the Aleutian invasion planning team was George Pearkes, a gallant Victoria Cross winner from the First World War and who later, as defence minister under John Diefenbaker, recommended the cancellation of the Arrow program.

Ironically, one of the Patricias who would fight at Kapyong and was aboard the *Martinez* had also fought in the Aleutians with the ship's slain namesake: Tommy Prince, an Ojibwe from just north of Winnipeg. Unbelievably brave, Prince fought later in Italy and France and ended the war as the most decorated soldier in Canadian history. However, it is unlikely that he and Joe Martinez ever actually crossed paths during the Alaskan campaign.

For three miserable agonizing weeks, the struggling little *Martinez* worked its way across the Pacific and its wretched and retching passengers bobbed like a cork in the rough weather. Few of the Patricias were convinced it was seaworthy. Only the rust, they said, was keeping the water out. Toilet facilities were crude. The food was inedible. The cooks sweated into the meals they were preparing.

"The weather was some of the worst in memory. Even the ship's crew were seasick," remembers Mike Czuboka. "I spent the first week in my bunk flat on my back and next to my rifle. The bunks were six deep and jammed together in the hold. The odour of unwashed bodies and feet was almost unbearable."[11]

John Bishop remembers the creaking of the hull convinced the soldiers they were headed straight for the bottom long before they'd ever make it to the battlefield. Even the captain was seasick.

"The hull developed a vertical crack along the bulkhead of our hold," he wrote. "In the roughest weather we could actually see it lengthening as the water leaked in. A warm soup of sea water and vomit sloshed back and forth every time the ship rolled, and when the ship heeled badly to our side it was over a foot deep."[12]

No one mentioned anything like this in those inspiring recruiting ads.

Only Smiley Douglas was (and is today) irrepressibly happy about everything, including the *Martinez*. For a twenty-year-old farm boy from little Elnora, Alberta, the voyage on this miserable troop ship was his greatest adventure and he was determined to enjoy it. "The ship was not so bad," he says now. "It didn't sink. What the hell, it stayed afloat didn't it? It was the only holiday I've ever had on the ocean."[13]

Smiley's bulldog refusal to be downhearted was to become remarkably evident later, at Kapyong.

On the way to Korea, a curious thing happened to the war-that-was-almost-over: suddenly it wasn't. Halfway into their journey, on October 25, the 2 PPCLI learned China was pouring in troops to save North Korea. No one could ever have dreamed it then, but the Chinese invasion had now destined the Patricias to their bleak hilltop in the Kapyong valley six months later.

The U.N. forces were suddenly reeling under the Chinese onslaught. An American army division and a marine division had been trapped in the snows of North Korean valleys, and had fought their way out with great bravery and tenacity and at great cost. Getting the men out had been a very close thing. The U.N. forces, led by the Americans, were able to slow the communist advance, but the perimeter was shrinking. Everyone able to carry a rifle was going to be needed, and the Americans were making desperate plans for the sea-sick, half-trained, untried, green Patricias from Canada to be sent straight to the front, which was getting closer by the hour.

The cushy, if boring, tedious, and definitely unglamorous, tour of occupation duty for 2 PPCLI was now certainly not going to happen. There would be a desperate scramble to turn it all around. Overnight, the Canadian modest occupation mission had quickly evolved into a highly dangerous, violent, and utterly unpredictable war against one of the biggest armies on earth.

Somewhere, Mackenzie King was saying "don't look at me."

The *Martinez* pulled into Pusan harbour, on Korea's southeast coast, on December 18. On the dock, a U.S. Army band played "If I Knew You Were Coming, I'd Have Baked a Cake." A group of young Korean schoolgirls waved flags as they lined the pier to welcome these strange and amiable young men who'd come across the world to fight for their country.

The curious Canadians soldiers, most of whom had never been far from home, were appalled by the dockside scene. They'd seen nothing like this in their lives. Korea was desperately poor at the best of times, but now it had been savaged by war. There was a certain aroma to Pusan the troops picked up while still a few miles out at sea — bodies were floating in the harbour. Squalor was everywhere: in the ruined buildings and warehouses, in wrecked vehicles, in the squatters' shacks of corrugated metal, on the streets clogged with rubble and rotting garbage, and in the eyes of orphaned kids in rags.

The Patricias, out of shape as they were, unsteady on their feet, and bewildered by this strange land, had finally arrived and set foot in their new home. They set up operations on an island in the harbour, and began to collect their equipment and devour American rations, which were delicious after the mysterious and unidentifiable offerings from the galleys of the *Martinez*.

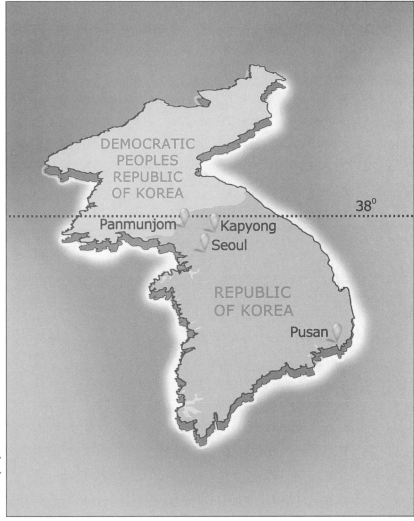

Korean Maps by Eric Foss and Manmeet Ahluwalia.

This map shows Pusan, South Korea's major port and where 2 PPCLI arrived; the South Korean capital, Seoul; nearby Kapyong; and Panmunjom, where armistice negotiations were eventually held that would end the war.

So there they were. The brand new 2nd Battalion, Princess Patricia's Canadian Light Infantry, an all-volunteer citizen's army from Canada, had arrived at last at their war. This is why they had signed on last summer. They'd caught up with Jack James's scoop. Let it begin … but not quite yet.

CHAPTER 3

A CITIZEN'S ARMY GOES TO WAR

The Americans, trying to stave off a catastrophe as the Chinese advanced further south, had made plans weeks before to send the Canadians straight to the front once they arrived. But as far as Jim Stone was concerned, this was not going to happen. Not a second time.

The ghosts of the Hong Kong debacle were still fresh in everyone's minds, since, only nine years earlier, poorly trained and unprepared Canadian soldiers had been sent to their deaths or imprisonment in a hopeless contest against the tough and well-trained Japanese. The Hong Kong fiasco haunted every step of the planning for Korea. Young Canadian soldiers would never again be sacrificed in some hopeless cause in a war in which Canada had little say. This time Canada would control the fate of its own troops, and of that, at least, Mackenzie King would have approved. During the Second World War he had insisted that Canadians fight in Canadian formations and would be led by Canadian commanders who would determine when their men were ready for action.

Stone had been specifically promised by Ottawa that his men would not go into combat until he was personally satisfied that they were ready for action. He had it in writing, literally, which turned out to be an extremely wise precaution.

A representative of American General "Johnnie" Walker, the overall commander in Korea, showed up to welcome Stone, but also to imperiously inform him that the situation was grave and the Patricias were needed at the front now. Trucks were on the way to pick up the men and carry them north to the sound of the guns, towards the Chinese. Stone balked, insisting his men were not ready for combat; they'd been prepared only for occupation duties, not for fighting, and needed eight weeks to toughen up.

The American shouted that the situation was desperate and the Canadians had come to fight, not to train. The granite-minded Stone refused to be bullied into a bad decision against his professional judgment.

Private Al Lynch from St. Catharines, Ontario, a runner at Stones' headquarters, was a fly on the wall at the confrontation.

"Two American officers were arguing with Stone," Lynch remembers. "They wanted Canadian troops sent into the line right away. They were arguing, and arguing loud. Stone just shouted: 'No way! They aren't going in.' The Americans just stormed out and went away."[1]

Stone had had enough of the deadlock. He demanded a plane to fly him to Walker up in Seoul to state his case in person. In Seoul, he first was met by a group of senior (and unsympathetic) members of Walker's staff.

"My position," Stone wrote in a letter years later, "was challenged by statements such as 'Your troops are trained as well as our reinforcements etc' which I admitted but tried to explain that we were not trained as formations; that we could function as sections (i.e. small units), but not as platoons, companies or a battalion. I was made so uncomfortable that eventually I produced my paper of authority (from Ottawa) which had the affect of stopping the inquisition."[2]

The next day Stone met Walker, who, with grace, backed off.

"General Walker had been well-briefed," Stone continued. "[He] mentioned something about not wanting to get mixed up in politics and was quite gracious in his dealing with a junior officer [Stone]. However, he insisted that my future actions would be observed by a US Major Fenstenmacher, presumably to ensure we were really training and not having a good time in the Korean paddy fields."[3]

However, Walker, Stone, and the Canadian cabinet seemed to tacitly understand that if outright disaster appeared probable at the front and the situation grew more perilous, then all bets were off and whatever troops were at hand, in whatever condition, would be thrown into the fray. But the front more-or-less stabilized — the Patricias weren't needed for now, at least, and the Canadians got down to the business of getting in shape for combat in this strange and wild land.

Walker was killed three days after his meeting with Stone, when his Jeep collided with a truck.

He was succeeded by Matthew Ridgway, a commander of great competence who is credited with turning the faltering war around. Americans have a knack for producing theatrical commanders. Ulysses Grant wore a mud-spattered uniform and chewed cigars. George Patton was spic-and-span and famously wore his trademark ivory-handled revolvers. MacArthur had his sunglasses and corncob pipe. Ridgway always had a couple of hand grenades dangling from his webbing.

With one eye on the calendar and another on the wavering front, where another Chinese offensive was being launched (Seoul fell, again), the Patricias arrived on New Year's Eve, near the village of Miryang, their new training base, about an hour's drive from Pusan. North Koreans were probing only about 75 miles away, and communist guerrillas were roaming the surrounding hills. It was a dangerous neighbourhood. This is where the Patricias would get battle-ready.

This was now Stone's army to whip into shape. These next few weeks were the key to the survival of the battalion. If Stone had not insisted on — and been granted — this breathing space for battle-hardening and conditioning, it is conceivable that the men of the 2nd Battalion would not have survived at Kapyong four months later.

Stone's men knew he would never squander their lives. John Bishop, then a lance corporal and in later life a lieutenant-colonel, says Stone was "a stubborn, single-minded bastard in whom everyone had confidence."[4] The soldiers and their colonel would, in the end, trust each other utterly. Stone later said the men who fought under him at Kapyong were the finest troops he'd ever commanded.

But the Canadians arrived at the war with the wrong training and the wrong weapons.

Korea was a country of steep hills and deep valleys. The objective would be to control those heights or knock the enemy off them. The Chinese and North Koreans had exactly the same idea. Later in the conflict it would become a war of patrols. At this early stage where there was manoeuvring, it was a war for the hills. Most of the Canadian infantry battle doctrine had been based on its fighting in northern Europe, among the hedgerows of Normandy in France, the canals and waterways of the Scheldt in Holland and Belgium, and in the thick forests of northern Germany. It had been a war of movement.

Korea was utterly unlike that. Korea, with its hills to the horizon, demanded soldiers in exceptional physical shape, carrying seventy pounds or more of gear on their backs for days at a time.

The outdated weapons they were issued were out-of-place. There would be occasional actions in which defending troops were swamped by human waves. Korea was also largely about smaller clashes: extremely violent, close-up, usually short-lived, and often at night. What was needed was plenty of firepower, which the Canadians did not have.

Initially, the plan was to issue the Patricias a mixture of American and British weapons and gear, but the battalion was being raised in a hurry, so it was decided that only using British equipment would cut training time. This was unfortunate, as events would prove.

The basic Canadian infantry weapon was the Lee-Enfield .303 rifle: an excellent, accurate, reliable firearm, and good for specialized work such as sniping (at which Canadians such as Ted Zuber excelled). But it was a bolt-action weapon. Each time a new round was to be fired, the rifle's "bolt" had to be operated. It had to be raised up, then pulled back to eject the spent brass casing, shoved forward to insert the next bullet into the firing chamber, and then the bolt was pushed downward, locking the mechanism into place. (At least it was an improvement on the infamous Ross Rifle in the First World War, which tended to either jam or send the bolt flying back into the face of the shooter.) Once the Lee-Enfield bolt was sent forward, the rifle was reloaded and ready to fire again — almost. First it had to be re-aimed all over again. It sounds easy enough to operate in the relative serenity of a target range, but it was a different matter entirely in the frenzy of combat when motors skills and dexterity can deteriorate, and as hoards of enemy soldiers swirl about your position, although some skilled marksmen could still get off forty shots a minute.

Still, the Lee-Enfield as the choice of weapon drastically reduced the firepower a platoon could bring to bear against the communists who used automatic weapons which fired as long as the trigger was pressed, or until it ran out of ammunition. The Canadians' sturdy but slow Lee-Enfields put them at a tremendous disadvantage against an enemy who would rush them in swarms.

PPCLI Museum and Archives.

2 PPCLI soldiers in defence at an unknown location in what appears to be an irrigation ditch crossing a rice paddy. Their bolt-action Lee-Enfield rifles can be clearly seen. Most of the battalion's clashes with the Chinese, who were armed with automatic weapons, were not in the open, as seen here, but high up in the ravines, gullies, and caves of the surrounding hills.

The Patricias knew they would be drastically outgunned, and it was commonplace for them to unofficially "acquire" U.S. automatics.

A Canadian favourite was a classic American gangster weapon, the Thompson submachine gun, the type made famous in Hollywood movies about Chicago mobs. The Thompson was heavy to carry around, hopelessly inaccurate at long range, but it fired a bullet about the size of the end of a grown man's thumb, had terrific "stopping power," and could send about 800 rounds a minute down the barrel. It was out of place at a sharpshooter's competition, but it was lethal for clearing rooms, ambushes, or any close-up work, the kind of fighting that was commonplace in Korea. If someone was hit by a Thompson, he went down and stayed down. It was the weapon of choice for Mike Levy, who used a Thompson he'd captured from the Chinese. Levy would later be at the centre of one of the most perilous moments at Kapyong.

Allowing troops to use unconventional and unauthorized weapons if they wanted to was quietly tolerated by the army brass on the assumption it was wisest to let soldiers fight with whatever gave them the greatest comfort and confidence.

Historically, one of the rationales that army bureaucrats have used over the years for being reluctant to issue semi-automatic weapons is that the men were just too unsophisticated and would become overexcited and jittery and start blazing away at anything, soon firing off all their ammunition. This ignored the fact that many of the soldiers were country boys who already knew a thing or two about firearms and hunting. There is more than a trace of class snobbery in the condescending army attitude. The not-so-subtle patronizing assumption is that it would take the reassuring presence and leadership of the officer class to steady up the nervous ordinary soldier. In other words, if the men were issued semi-automatics, they could not be trusted, on their own, to use what's termed "fire control." Such reservations did not stop American or Soviet armies in the Second World War from lavishly arming their troops with automatic weapons. Such increased firepower, they reasoned, gave their individual soldiers an immense destructive capacity and also increased their confidence. And American and Soviet soldiers did not, in fact, run out of ammunition just because of the particular weapons they were using.

The Patricias were lucky they were not annihilated at Kapyong with their out-gunned, slow-firing, bolt-action Lee-Enfields. That they survived is due, in part, not to the weapons Ottawa made them use, but to their own steely cool-headedness. Finally, in the late 1950s, Canada's military figured out what was needed on a modern battlefield and adopted a semi-automatic infantry rifle. It was the FN, designed by Fabrique Nationale, a Belgian arms company. Since 1984, the standard Canadian infantry weapon has been the C7, a semi-automatic based on the American M16 designed by Colt.

In Korea, Canadian soldiers also regarded British anti-tank guns as useless, preferring American bazookas and recoilless rifles and mortars, which could also be used to knock out gun emplacements and bunkers. The American-designed Browning .50-calibre heavy machine gun was also a popular weapon. It fires a bullet the size of a large carrot, is capable of great devastation, and has been used in bombers for protection against attacking fighters. Today it is still the heavy machine gun preferred by most armies. It was the handful of "50 cals" that were crucial in saving the 2 PPCLI's headquarters from being overrun at Kapyong.

In a curious and unusual reversal of preferences, U.S. forces preferred Canadian hand grenades, which were believed to have greater explosive power. But unlike in the movies, real hand grenades do not blow up tanks and destroy buildings. They are used as "anti-personnel" devices, to clear rooms, bunkers, or trenches, or to catch troops in the open. The most perilous moment for the user is when he must expose himself for an instant to hurl it at the enemy. There is also a great incentive, obviously, for him to have quick access to cover or risk becoming his own casualty.

The Patricias were issued the famous British-style helmet, the so-called "tin hat," which had its origins in the First World War. It was universally hated. It offered the wearer almost no protection and was almost instantly "lost" by its Canadian owners. There are virtually no photographs at any point in the war of Canadians wearing their British helmets. They much preferred American G.I. helmets, but mostly they simply settled for soft cloth caps, toques, occasionally berets, or often no headwear at all in combat.

Mike Czuboka's reaction to the Canadian issue helmets was typical: "We never wore our helmets. They were heavy and uncomfortable. We just threw them away. We wore balaclavas or peaked hats."[5]

PPCLI Museum and Archives.

A 2 PPCLI patrol crosses a rice paddy, the men laden down with what they would live with: weapons, ammunition, a blanket, and rain gear.

For most Canadians in Korea, their Canadian-issue gear was second rate, but their winter clothing was among the best that any army used in the Korean winter. John Bishop: "We were a winterized people. Only the Chinese were dressed for winter weather better than we were. 'We were Canadians,' we said. 'We can do this better than anyone one else.'"[6]

Czuboka says, "Our Canadian arctic gear, our parks and wind pants, they were really comfortable and warm. The pants, however, made a loud noise when we walked (a bad idea on night patrols). And our hobnailed boots were heavy and also noisy. We would never give our parkas away, but we'd use American boots whenever we could scrounge them."[7]

To an infantryman, his feet are second only to his rifle in his list of life-saving priorities. To a foot soldier, boots are a very big deal. Al Lynch: "We had good clothing, but our boots eventually fell off our feet. In the freezing rain our boots and the feet inside got soaked. The boots froze. We'd take them off and couldn't get them back on. So I got myself some good American boots."[8]

Eventually, Canada actually did issue an automatic weapon. It was the Sten gun and would have been something of a joke, except that soldiers' lives often depended on it. But it was found wanting, to put it

58

mildly. They were inexpensive, easy to mass produce, and simple to work ... if they worked. They were much used by resistance fighters in the Second World War, but sadly, they were a pathetic, unreliable, inaccurate little submachine gun that could be guaranteed to jam at the worst possible moment. They could also be guaranteed to go off accidentally at the worst possible moment. The troops hated them and when issued the weapon, in Mike Czuboka's words, "we just ignored them."[9]

Canadians wanted the Thompsons or almost any American weapon, and according to Czuboka, it was free enterprise in action. "A lot of guys got themselves American .45-calibre pistols (which fired the same ammunition as the Thompsons). The Americans would supply us with the ammo. You could get yourself an American carbine for a bottle of whiskey. Hard liquor was the currency we would use it to buy this stuff with."[10]

Canadian troops had beer and booze, but no modern weapons. American troops had modern weapons but no beer or booze. So unofficial deals were made; a sort of early free trade agreement.

Don Hibbs had a genius for negotiations.

> A lieutenant, myself, and another corporal went down to Pusan with our Jeep to do some trading. What my Colonel or my Major wanted was a Jeep trailer, and two walkie-talkies, that was what our project was. So we went downtown to Pusan and I had to look around, I found an American general headquarters, and I went in there to the Sergeant on duty. He asked me what have I got to trade, and I got a bottle of rum out of the jeep. I said, "I need a trailer."
>
> He says, "I'll get you one, I'll get you one."
>
> So I gave him the bottle, I got the two walkie-talkies, the two 45's [pistols]. And about ten minutes later he comes driving up with a two-and-a-half-ton truck with a two-and-a-half-ton trailer on the back, and says "There's your trailer."
>
> And I said, "I can't pull that. I have only got a Jeep."
> He said, "Well, take the truck." So I did.

We went for every single bit of American equipment we could grab. For a bottle of whiskey you could
get a carbine and all the ammo you wanted. The Lee-
Enfield: definitely wrong weapon! Totally! In battle you
could hear them stop, cock and fire again. A lot of guys
are dead because we'd be overrun. They'd pull the trigger
and it went "click." We had terrible weapons. Everyone
had a sidearm [a handgun] or a Tommy gun or a carbine
that they'd bought off the yanks. I had a two .45s [Colt
automatic pistols]. I looked like Patton.[11]

Bill Chrysler preferred American weapons, but was one of the
minority that also wanted U.S. winter clothing: "I wore a lot of American
stuff. Their clothing [was] heavier and warmer. Our own clothing was
leftovers from World War Two. Also, we all tried to get American weapons."[12] Chrysler's specialty was the 50-calibre machine gun.

———

The six-week breathing space at Miryang granted to the Patricias by
the American commander, Matthew Ridgway, was not a rest break.
The Canadian base was around 100 miles from the front, but the area
was rife with communist guerrillas. Miryang was near an apple orchard
and thankfully not near rice paddies, with their strange accompanying
odours. And at least Miryang was away from the squalor and stench of
Pusan. Jim Stone began forging his army.

Training was tough, thorough, and unrelenting. Stone's simple message to his men was that soft, out-of-condition soldiers would die in this
tough, brutal war. Fit, motivated, disciplined soldiers, who could fight
as a team, would live. Training conditions were to resemble actual combat as much as possible so the psychological transition from training to
fighting would be as seamless as possible.

To deal with troublemakers, a punishment camp was set up con-
sisting of a tent surrounded by barbed bar. Stone said it would be the
toughest punishment camp since the days of Admiral Horatio Nelson
(although by the draconian punishment standards of his day, Nelson was
a moderate and not regarded as a "lasher").

This time at Miryang was a vital weeding-out process,

Eventually, about sixty men would be considered unfit psychologically and physically for combat operations and were sent home. Better that misfits and troublemakers be discovered now, and not later when it was too late, when Chinese infantry would be storming into their positions.

Stone believed discipline issues should handled promptly and publicly. One group of soldiers stole some of the battalion's beer ration. The thieves were caught.

"I paraded that group in front of the whole battalion and gave them hell," Stone wrote later. "'These men stole your beer' I told them. 'Your beer, not mine. The same kind of guy who steals your beer back here will steal your water at the front line.' Then I gave each of them 14 days."[13] It was Stone's way of driving home the message they were all dependent on each other.

To show he meant business and that war was no lark, Stone told his troops not to expect any medals. He didn't believe in them. Captain Murray Edwards remembers Stone's lecture: "One of the things that made us unhappy was when Stone paraded us and told us 'You're all volunteers. You're being paid for what you do and I'm not recommending medals for anyone.'"[14]

It was an odd tone to set at the start of a perilous campaign when the men expected a pep talk. As it turned out, five medals were awarded after Kapyong, including one to Stone himself.

Sergeant Alex Sim, who'd fought in the Second World War and reenlisted for Korea, deeply admired Stone, but was constantly puzzled about what made the man tick. "Stone," Sim says now, "was a great leader and a great commander. He was a great tactician. Nothing bothered him. But he was kind of a strange person."[15]

Stone emphasized to his soldiers to get off the roads. He felt American and South Korean troops were in deplorable physical (and sometimes psychological) shape, were too reliant on road-bound tanks and air cover, and were reluctant to leave their trucks or stray from the beaten path. This was not Stone's way of war. Get up in the hills, he urged. That is where the enemy is. Stone taught his men they must essentially take along everything they would fight with and not to depend on relying for help from other units or tanks or planes. Go for the high ground, he

Photo by Hub Gray.

Members of 2 PPCLI patrol railway line near a destroyed railway station, about two weeks after Kapyong.

would urge, drawing on his combat savvy, fine-tuned in the mountains of Italy; go along ridges, with platoons leap-frogging each other. It was an aggressive style of fighting, articulated by an aggressive commander. Stone and the U.S. Marines fought a very similar, take-the-fight-to-the-enemy type of war. Infiltrators would always be a risk, but a calculated one that could be dealt with. Just get up into those hills and keep moving. As Lincoln's favourite commander, Ulysses Grant, lectured his officers: stop worrying about what the other guy is going to do; make him worry about what you're going to do. Jim Stone would have been right at home with Grant, Rommel, Patton, Stalin's favourite marshal, Georgiy Zhukov, or Churchill's favourite innovative (and highly eccentric and brooding) commander, Orde Wingate.

As an indication of the haste with which the battalion had been raised and sent off to war, a rifle range was set up only in early February. For many of the Patricias, it was the first time they'd actually fired their weapons.

Time and energy would be spent guerrilla hunting, even when training. About 8,000 guerrillas were estimated to be operating in the South at the time. The immediacy of the threat was driven home when two neighbouring New Zealand soldiers in a Jeep were wounded in an ambush, with two others killed and mutilated.

The incident turned into the first combat mission of the Canadian army in the Korean War.

Captain Murray Edwards, in his private memoir on his Korean experiences, details the Patricias' initial encounter in fighting this war that still had another two years to run: "When they [the two New Zealanders] didn't arrive, a search was mounted. The Jeep was found with the driver dead from bayonet wounds."[16] The man had been stripped, beaten, and stabbed repeatedly through the throat. The second man had his arms bound, but his legs were unhindered. The Chinese then sliced off a hand at the wrist and left him to wander off through the woods as he lost blood with each step and with each heartbeat. The Patricias followed the red path.

"A trail of blood led to an abandoned Korean house where the Warrant Officer was found, his hands tied behind him. They had cut off one hand and left him to bleed to death. He had made his way to the house looking in vain for help."[17]

Soldiers expect to encounter much cruelty in combat, but this savagery was unexpected and incomprehensible to the Patricias.

Three days later there was a second attack, this time on a 2 PPCLI platoon, and a Patricia was wounded by a sniper. The war now was on their doorstep, even though they were still in training and supposedly out of harm's way. Stone, ever the man of action, sent B Company (later to be the first to receive the brunt of the Chinese attack at Kapyong) off in hot pursuit. This was to be 2 PPCLI's baptism of fire.

Taking with them little more than their rifles, ammunition, and some food, they climbed a series of craggy hills where the guerrillas were last seen, searched deserted villages, found nothing, and then climbed ever higher, scouring any caves they came across, and still found no trace of their elusive enemy. Night came and the men prepared to spend it in the open, digging a defence position where they were, when someone spotted figures moving across the skyline less than a mile away. They opened fire, wounding some guerrillas, but decided not to pursue them in the dark over terrain the enemy knew well. So they spent the night on the 2,700-foot-high hilltop.

It was February and the temperatures were low, but the men's spirits were high. This is, after all, why they had come to Korea. They set off again on the hunt at first light, coming across food left behind, some weapons, and a blood trail. Continuing the pursuit, they called for help from C Company, came across the guerrillas hiding in nearby caves and fields, and flushed them out. Many managed to escape, but two were killed and several were wounded.

"They killed several, including one who later proved to be their 2 IC [second-in-command]," wrote Murray Edwards. "The rest broke and ran. Continuing to the top, we found a cave complete with a printing press and a number of papers. One of which, when interpreted, were a list of locals who were to be 'eliminated.' A pursuit was organized … one of the boys in my platoon spotted a wallet on the ground. It proved to belong to the dead warrant officer. What really hit me was to open it up and see a photograph of his wife and children."[18]

The Patricias, in their first combat, had been tenacious. The hunt for the other guerrillas went on for two more days before it was ended. The battalion's War Diary noted: "Everyone in the Battalion is eager to get into the action. All the companies are envious of B Company and are eagerly awaiting for what they hope will be their turn."[19]

The men had shown initiative and zeal in this, their first test, especially considering they had not completed their training. It was at this clash that it was first noticed the Canadian-issue boots would fall apart after a few days of rugged use over tough terrain.

The Patricias got an early sample from their American allies on how combat can numb normal human sensitivities. These grim little nuggets from history often come to us from personal memories jotted down for family and friends, not in scholarly works, journalistic accounts, or official documents. But these private writings can provide a vivid picture of Canada at war through small, telling details.

In one early incident, the Patricias could not get over the cold detachment of the American soldiers to the fate of a fellow countryman who had just been killed.

Edwards, in the series of vignettes he wrote down for his family, describes an attack on a hill, so obscure and unimportant now that he can no longer recall its name, if it was ever even important enough to have one, or how many casualties were suffered. They were coming under increasingly intense fire, but were getting backup from some daring American pilots. Swooping in very low, and highly vulnerable to ground fire, the flyers were taking great risks to help the Patricias.

"We were supported in this action," writes Edwards, "by four American Mustang fighters. Their first low-level attack went home, but on the second pass the left wing of the fourth plane suddenly flew off and the plane, already very low, spiralled out of sight over the road and disappeared, followed by the sound of an explosion and a dense cloud of black smoke."[20]

Some of the Patricias went off to see what they could discover and soon came across the plane wreckage and the pilot's body trapped inside.

> We found the plane and pilot. Our medical officer, Captain Fitzgerald, found his identification. His name was MacDonald. [Fitzgerald] then had his body moved by Jeep ambulance to an American Army unit on our left flank.
>
> Then, unbelievably, we received a message from the American unit to return and pick up MacDonald's body. When our people arrived and asked "Why?" they were informed: "He doesn't belong to us. He's Air Force."[21]

If it weren't for Murray Edwards's sad notes, no one would ever know the story of the brave American flyer known only as MacDonald who had died that day trying to help Canadian soldiers fighting beneath his wingtips.

Edwards writes of another lesson in numbing sensitivities. He was stunned when his men went to the New Zealand field headquarters to return the wallet and photos of the dead warrant officer mutilated and killed by the Chinese.

"I still don't understand the reception I had," wrote Edwards. "After telling [the New Zealand adjutant] who I was and how one of my Privates had found the wallet, all I got was 'OK, leave it on the desk.' And he carried on reading his paper."[22]

Edwards, with a diarist's eye for a telling detail, also chronicled the wiles soldiers have been using to cope with the anxiety of combat since the time of Troy. As quartermaster in charge of all supplies, from ammunition to food, he had been safeguarding the battalion's six gallons of rum rations. "This was April," Edwards writes. "[We] had been through three bitter months of cold weather and not once did Colonel Stone authorize an issue. After Kapyong he finally relented and I opened the first of those jugs that I had to zealously guarded. And what came out?! Water! A close examination showed that a hypodermic needle had been inserted through the cork and siphoned off the rum and replaced it with water."[23]

The rum mystery, like the mysterious case of the key to the strawberry locker in the classic Second World War novel *The Caine Mutiny*, was never solved.

By mid-February, eight months after the North Korean invasion, the Patricias were ready to go into combat at last. Stone felt his men were now tough enough and had enough tactical skill to hold their own against the North Koreans and the Chinese. They became part of the 27th Commonwealth Brigade and would fight alongside English and Scottish troops, Australians and New Zealanders, and attached to them was a medical unit from India.

It was a two-day ordeal to the front, moving by truck through the mountains, around winding treacherous curves, and through snow and sleet. Finally the trucks ground to a halt, the Patricias got out and marched another five miles overland to their front lines. They were loaded down with packs and supplies. It was an exhausting ordeal.

Later in the war, with stalemated front lines, patrolling, and sniping, and artillery exchanges with little real manoeuvring, the war degenerated into a duel of grinding attrition, with occasional attacks by thousands of massed Chinese troops. It was the style of combat that suits armies with massive resources of manpower that can afford to be indifferent to high losses. This was not combat that suited the culture of the highly mechanized, but casualty sensitive, "Western" armies. This way of war was ideal for the Chinese. But the stalemate and attrition came later. In this early stage of the Korean War, the 2 PPCLI stage, there was still movement and manoeuvring, with one side trying to get around the flanks of the other, or fight to control those hilltops.

In this image, the 2 PPCLI is seen crossing a log bridge over a river in February 1951. The soldier on the right appears to be Private Jon Hoskins.

As the Chinese slowly withdrew northward, they left behind pockets of skirmishers and thousands of roving bands of guerrillas.

The Patricias arrived at the front on February 17. The next morning, almost three feet of snow had been dumped on their positions. On the 21st, with renewed fighting spirit and higher morale among the American troops, "Operation Killer" was launched to bring U.N. forces closer to the 38th parallel. For the Canadians just getting started in this war, the operation's code name was a spooky omen.

CHAPTER 4

DEATH IN THE SNOW

The Patricias' role in Operation Killer was to attack Hill 404, as the blizzard continued to sweep across their front. They found the Chinese had broken off contact and abandoned their hilltop trenches, and there was no combat that day. But the Chinese had left behind a grim lesson that has been re-taught through the ages as young men go off to war: Never for even a second get forgetful, and never dream for a moment that you are in a normal world rather than where you really are.

"It was a massacre," recalls Kim Reynolds. "They were half dressed. They tried to get out of their sleeping bags. They didn't make it."[1]

The Patricias had stumbled across a group of American soldiers who'd literally been caught napping. They paid a terrible price for their sloppy discipline.

"They were naked," remembers Mike Czuboka. "The Chinese stripped them. Whenever they killed an American they loved to get their clothes. So they took the shirts of these guys — their books, everything. It seemed half their army was equipped with American equipment. I didn't eat very much for three or four days. I'd never seen a dead person before in my life. Now I saw dozens of them."[2]

The dead G.I.s had probably been shipped over from occupation duty in Japan and clearly were ill-trained and unprepared for combat. Apparently they had eaten their rations, casually posted a couple of guards, then undressed and bedded down in their sleeping bags without posting proper sentries. It was unbelievably lackadaisical and negligent in a combat zone.

"All this had been observed by the Chinese sitting on the high ground," writes Murray Edwards. "Just after midnight they came down, killed the two guards and then most of the patrol while they struggled to get out of those sleeping bags."[3]

Sixty years later, coming across these frozen American bodies is still a searing memory for the young Canadians. Everyone who was there has an image in their minds of the ghastly sight that is as vivid now as it was then. Alex Sim remembers:

> It was our first time in the line. We were just moving up. I was thinking, "Here I am about to move into our first position and I haven't seen any sign of the enemy." I thought it was kind of strange.
>
> Then we came across this ninety-eight-member Negro reconnaissance team. They'd scouted out some villages, and being novices they didn't post sentries, or very many. There was nobody left alive. They all climbed in their sleeping bags and went to sleep. It was a terrible sight. Some were in undershorts and barefoot. They were stretched all along the road. They were lined up like ten pins. Some never got out of the sleeping bags. Some had a rifle in one hand and helmet in the other. I said to my brother: "There you are. There's your introduction to war."[4]

The Chinese had carefully planned the slaughter and had set up machine guns covering the snow-covered road to mow down the few who managed to get free of their sleeping bags in time.

It looked like something from a cheap horror movie.

> I didn't see any trenches to suggest they'd taken even rudimentary precautions against attack. The village's buildings were charred and still smouldering, and straw from roofs and stores of cattle feed were still burning. The fires may have been caused during the attack, or set deliberately afterwards as a message to peasants who might be tempted to harbour UN soldiers.

The bodies close to the buildings were charred, as if roasted on a spit. Others further away, posed in grotesque positions, were frozen solid like carcasses in a walk-in freezer, and a couple of corpses were rigged as bobby traps.[5]

There were no whites among the bodies. The U.S. armed forces did not begin to desegregate until that fall. The horrified Patricias concluded the dead Americans were support troops who'd just delivered supplies to the front lines and were on the return trip to the rear, assuming they were now out of harm's way. They'd halted for the night in this deadly spot, only about a mile from the front and in an area teeming with guerrillas. The almost complete absence of security in such a dangerous neighbourhood seemed unbelievably lax to the Canadians.

Don Hibbs recalls the smallest terrible details: "Bodies were laying everywhere; half in their sleeping bags. Half were naked."[6]

Some apparently were able to fight back for a few frantic moments.

"One dead guy was leaning over a Jeep windshield, trying to man a machinegun," says Hibbs. "He was up to his knees in empty shells. His name, 'Lewis,' was on his helmet. Guys had their sleeping bagger zippers caught. They were trapped. There were no quick releases. They were trying to unzip them. Guys were bayoneted and shot right through their sleeping bags."

Hibbs remembers they were ordered to hurry up and finish their lunch.

"I thought, lunch? I'm sitting eating lunch looking around and seeing like all these dead men that have been killed the night before. Rigor mortis hadn't even set in. And I thought this is terrible, you know, and that's when I wrote my mother a letter and said 'Farewell, I'll never see you again.'"[7]

"I remember that in my dreams," recalls John Bishop. "Seeing those fellows, frozen; booby-trapped grenades between legs and under their arm pits. It was a grisly sight."[8]

Seasoned war correspondent, Bill Boss of the Canadian Press news agency, filed a report on the massacre, somehow eluding American censors, who were furious because they were trying to keep the disaster secret. Boss's story broke it to the world.

Ever the tough professional, Stone saw this tragedy as an opportunity. It was an object lesson to his men in survival. Stone paraded his troops at the spot where the Americans had died, and bluntly told them he was taking away their sleeping bags. They'd have to make do with blankets. After what they'd just seen, Stone was saving their lives.

"Stone marched us right past those dead Americans," remembers Al Lynch, from the B.C. interior. "He made us look at them. They were just lying there along the road. Then he marched us a little further down and said: 'Turn in your sleeping bag. Here's one blanket.'"[9]

How long could he sleep in one blanket? "Oh, a month, maybe six weeks."

> Stone just said "Take your sleeping bags and throw them on the truck. You're not going to be sleeping in them. Just sleep in your clothes in the bottom of a trench."
>
> Well, we had good coats, a mesh undershirt that could breathe, a shirt, a sweater, a tunic, and heavy sheep-lined parkas. We were good for going into the hills for three weeks or a month. I never took boots off. My socks all rotted.[10]

Miserably uncomfortable perhaps, but at least Don Hibbs did not die.

Bill Chrysler: "The Colonel took our bags and gave us a blanket. I thought, 'Do I want a bayonet in the throat or bullet in my head?' I don't think so. I was determined I was not going to be caught in sleeping bag like these guys were."[11]

If those American troops had been commanded by Jim Stone, they would not have died that night on a godforsaken road in Korea.

Kim Reynolds: "It was a lesson. As long as we were in the front line, we never did sleep in sleeping bags. We always had sentries. Either 50 or 25 percent of us were on sentry duty for two hours; then we'd rotate. And we never took off our boots. And we never put parka hoods up. I went out with just a blanket for five or six weeks."[12]

Stone imposed a Spartan routine. There were few grumblers.

John Bishop: "Stone took away our goddamn sleeping bags. I just had blanket. One day or two days before Kapyong [in a rest area] we got sleeping bags. But I then was only in a sleeping bag once till I left for home."[13]

"We became sort of a brown color. Like dirt," says Kim Reynolds. "There was no chance to be spic-and-span. We had to shave, but that was about the extent of it."[14]

They were a curious-looking bunch. Look at their photographs from the time, as they stare out at us from sixty years ago. They seemed like so un-serious a fighting force: bareheaded half the time, wearing a toque the other half; armed to the teeth with an exotic assortment of grenades and knives and bayonets and shovels and ammunition and guns, much of it not exactly government-issue, to put it mildly. There was a deceptive informality to their style and a sort of amateur-night-at-the-war feel to it all, with their improvised uniforms, baggy trousers, tousled hair, berets and balaclavas, dangling cigarettes, the occasional bottles of beer (unheard of in American units), and their strange array of weapons (which were always clean, well-oiled, and in pristine condition).

They resembled some blend of Che Guevara's guerrillas and the Israeli army in their casual citizens' army style. One Patricia said "We looked like bums." Except that they weren't.

They were horrified, but not terrified, by the scene of the American massacre. Their tough training was paying off. They were, by now, in superb physical shape. They were highly motivated, and had soaring confidence. For an army composed largely of amateurs, they felt as professional as any in Korea.

They wanted adventure and they were going to get it.

The weather was miserable. So dreadful were the conditions that soldiers wondered why anyone would want to live in Korea at all.

Pierre Berton, writing in *Maclean's* magazine described the deep snow, then rain, then sleet, and then frozen soil: "The men's parkas, battledress and underwear became soaked and frozen. They crouched in a foot of water. Blankets turned into sopping grey."[15]

At this stage in the war, there was public interest and press coverage. At the front, there was action and movement, attacks and raids. There was something exciting to write about

But this was early in the war and Canadians were only just into the fighting and the folks back home wanted to know how their boys were doing. But later in the war, when it turned into a gruelling stalemate, with the two sides locked in their trenches and the front lines scarcely moving, the public's interest faded. Men were still dying, but unless you were a relative, nothing seemed to have happened over there in Korea. So the Korean War started to become the Forgotten War not in the years after, but while it was still being fought. Men would return home only to be asked where they'd been the past while; no one had seen them around. But this lay in the future. In early 1951, the war was hot. And it was still hot "news."

After the gruesome discovery of the dead Americans, the Patricias continued making their plodding way northward, and upward, moving along near the tops of the hills. Patricias were critical of the quality of many of the regular U.S. Army troops they encountered. Most of the American G.I.s were draftees, wished they were home, and hated to leave the roads and valleys and protection of their tanks. The Patricias, however, did have respect for the U.S. Marines they encountered. The men, like their leader Jim Stone, found the marines to be aggressive, like the Patricias. They preferred to fight to control the tops of hills and avoid the valleys, like the Patricias. And they were volunteers, like the Patricias.

Enemy gunfire would claim its victims, but so too would the sheer harshness of the weather and wildness of the terrain. The snow-swept Korean hills in winter were treacherous, dangerous places. The slopes became slippery and there were casualties. Two men loaded down with their packs and gear lost their footing and tumbled down the icy slopes. Each such mishap subtracted from the men available for combat. They were casualties as much as men who were felled by gunfire. Digging in for the night through several feet of snow, the rest settled down at the 1,200-foot level. It was February 21. It was a cold and hungry night, but morale was high. The next day they were to attack a feature known only as Hill 444.

Kapyong would be the 2nd Battalion's finest hour, but that was still weeks away and the road to their most famous battle was marked by a string of nasty, vicious encounters that no one recalls now, but each produced its tally of body bags. The Patricias began taking casualties almost from the start of combat operations.

The hills to keep track of as the Patricias fought their way north are Hills 444, 419, and 532.

Private Jon Hoskins, 2 PPCLI, during the advance up Hill 419, February 24, 1951, a few weeks before Kapyong. One of the most famous Canadian images to come out of the Korean War, this iconic photograph shows what the men who fought at Kapyong actually looked like in combat. The Battalion was not a spic-and-span, parade ground unit, but a practical fighting force. Note the informality of the soldiers' dress and the lack of a helmet. In his right chest pocket are magazines the soldiers carried for the Bren light machine-gunners, and in his hand is his own Lee-Enfield rifle.

The names of these forgettable landmarks became blurred. Which hill was which soon lost much meaning. They all looked monotonously alike and the troops who fought on them would be hard-pressed to tell one from the other a few days later. They were identified by their eleva-

PPCLI Museum and Archives.

tion numbers and imbedded in the men's memories only so long as they were that day's objective. Then, as the troops would move on, Hill number such and such would be forgotten and there'd be another hill to be attacked, also soon to be nameless and featureless, and then another.

As night came on the 21st, Hill 444 was given no more thought than the countless ones that came before. But Hill 444 would be remembered for a while, at least. So would its neighbour, Hill 419. The next day would be a bloody day.

The Patricias were advancing up a valley when they came under machine gun fire from 444.

The Canadians swept aside the Chinese opposition, but sustained their first battle casualties. It was a costly operation: four men killed in one day. This was not like guerrilla hunting.

In the official history, this nasty fight for Hill 444 in which four Canadians gave their lives is dismissed in one thin sentence: "Major George's 'C' Company sustained the unit's first battle casualties in a two-platoon attack on Hill 444, when it lost four killed and one wounded."[16] And that's it.

But here's what it was really like to have been there. Follow along as Corporal John Bishop takes us through a rice paddy with his platoon: "I was soaked to the skin and the sheer effort of pulling my feet out of the ankle deep sludge on the path took a toll … we slogged along through mud and slush all that day, up and over each spur that ran down into the valley, only to climb the next one and the next."[17]

That's the numbing exhaustion that's absent from the official account, which also doesn't capture the terror of feeling the rush of displaced air made by high-velocity bullets whizzing by.

"I heard the distant staccato pop-popping of machine guns ahead of us, as tracers started whining all around us. Seeing those darts of light heading for me in lazy parabolas, I followed my instinct and dropped to my belly right there in the open, behind a foot-high mud wall at the edge of the rice paddy that was my only cover. As the tracers zipped past me like fireflies, I lay in the muck feeling very naked."[18]

Bishop lay there, as did the other green young soldiers under fire for the first time, wishing they were somewhere else and waiting for someone, somewhere, to tell them what to do.

In charge of this platoon there should have been an officer — a lieu-tenant. On this day, thankfully, it was a sergeant, Tommy Prince, an Ojibwe from Manitoba who became a legend in the Second World War with the Devil's Brigade and would become one all over again with the 2 PPCLI in Korea, and yet again when he came back later with 3 PPCLI. He was, perhaps, Canada's greatest soldier.

Tommy Prince got the platoon moving again.

"I couldn't see him, but I was sure that by this time he was up with the forward section spotting the source of the tracers, fixing them in his mind and sizing up the situation," writes Bishop. "The next thing I know he was up and running, waving us forward. In an instant I was on my feet calling to my section. The whole platoon leapt up and made a dash for-ward and down the slope in front, into dead ground and safety. As I ran shuffling forward weighted down by seventy pounds of packs and kit, I didn't even notice the burden ... and I knelt there gasping, wondering about our next move."[19]

The Patricias then pressed on to Hill 419, which was also to be a meat grinder.

Two platoons were sent on what should have been a traditional advance, where one group gives cover while the second advances, and they then leapfrog each other. This was the traditional infantry small unit tactic, battle-proven in Europe in the last war. But here in Korea the val-leys and ravines made movement difficult, restricting advances to single-file, breaking the momentum of an advance, and making the men easy targets. The Chinese, with their automatic weapons and machine guns, made this an expensive operation and the Canadian attack stalled. Four dead, for virtually no gain. Some enemy positions were taken, but the attack had stalled. They dug in for the night.

At nine o'clock the next morning, the Patricias moved out again. They were shaken when an American airstrike mistakenly hit Hill 444, just behind them, which they'd cleared the previous day. The U.S. flyers were using napalm, a jellied explosive invented at Harvard University, which bursts into flames on impact and sticks to what it hits. It was much used in the South Pacific during the Second World War, so many American troops were familiar with its results. But to most Canadians it was a new and strangely awful weapon.

With the smoking Hill 444 at their backs, the Patricias started climbing. It took C Company an hour and a half to make their way to the top ridges of Hill 419, inching along, when the Chinese opened fire again. Two men were killed outright and a third wounded. The attack stalled. Over the next seven hours they made two more attempts, but never made it.

Finally, as daylight was fading, they called it off, bringing down five of their dead and five wounded. D Company then attacked from another direction, also got nowhere, and gave up after losing one killed and three wounded. It had been a dreadful mission so far: six killed, eight wounded, and the Chinese still held the hill.

At dawn on the 24th, they tried yet another push. New Zealand artillery pounded Hill 419, and Americans dropped more napalm. Again, the nature of the landscape allowed men to advance only a section (ten men) at a time, making it difficult for an infantry attack to build momentum. The Patricias took fire from their front and from both sides.

The Company commander, Captain J.G. Turnbull, recalled: "Although we called down mortars artillery and air rockets, the Chinese were still there when we attacked … Never in Italy or Germany were we under fire as intense as that. It was incredible. It chopped off bush briar at the six-inch level."[20]

This was beginning to look a lot like First World War combat on a smaller scale: assaults against a well-entrenched enemy, blazing machine-gun fire, heavy losses, the attackers going back to where they began, leaving everyone more or less where they were at the start. It was turning into a war of attrition that only played to the strengths of the Chinese, with their massive sources of manpower and apparent indifference to casualties.

The attacks by Australians, trying to take a neighbouring hill, and the 2 PPCLI were sensibly called off — something that never occurred to the British commander Field Marshall Douglas Haig, whose men had been squandered in the mud at Passchendaele, where an earlier generation of Patricias had been thrown away.

For the first time the Canadians used Korean porters to bring them their food supplies and ammunition. Porters were often the only way to get provisions up to Canadians high on hilltops and far from passable roads. They were called "rice burners," and later some journalists claimed the Canadians were condescending towards these loyal

A section of ten men of 2 PPCLI moves forward to renew their attack on Hill 419. The men have only been in combat about two weeks, but already they have the look and feel of seasoned veterans. The Patricias much preferred the superior American weapons, equipment, and boots, but they did favour Canadian winter clothing. Note the barren, mountainous terrain the Patricias fought in.

and hard working locals. But mostly the Patricias were genuinely fond of these men and young boys, who shared the perils of living at the front. Some were trapped at Kapyong along with the Canadian soldiers and were there throughout the battle, little noticed or remembered by history.

The Australians and the Patricias aggressively patrolled their fronts for the next three days. On the 27th, a lone Australian platoon finally took its hill, 614, with the help of mortar fire and air support. That made neighbouring Hill 419 untenable for the Chinese and they withdrew. The next day the Patricias took possession and discovered the stripped and frozen bodies of four Canadians. The Chinese apparently had brought them back to their positions with their own dead to get their clothing and weapons.

The Patricias were taken out of the line and went into reserve for rest and re-equipping. It had been a gruelling slugfest. In a week, ten men had been killed and twenty wounded.

The Chinese were not at all like they'd been told. A British War Office report stated: "There is nothing surprising about the enemy; their concealment, mobility, poor marksmanship, stamina and boldness [are] all characteristic of the Japanese."[21]

No soldier who'd actually fought the Chinese agreed with this report that was so detached from reality.

"The Chinese? They were damned good soldiers," says Don Hibbs. "They would fight regardless of the outcome. A thousand could be coming. We'd keep shooting. They'd keep coming."[22]

John Bishop: "They were experts at patrols and at night fighting. They were a serious enemy, although their lives didn't mean much to their commanders."[23]

The Canadians saw their Chinese foes as brave and tough, but they lacked independent initiative, waiting instead for specific orders. If things went wrong, and in war things always go wrong, Canadian soldiers are taught to use their own judgment if there are no orders and to assume command if a leader is killed or wounded. Sergeant Tommy Prince, for example, often acted as a platoon leader, normally the role of a lieutenant. Individual Chinese soldiers did not respond well to the unexpected and were not conditioned to act on their own, or they were afraid they'd be punished if they acted without formal official approval. This is a sure way for an attack to bog down if the leaders are killed.

"We respected the Chinese soldiers," says Mike Czuboka, "but I don't think they were exceptionally competent. Their main tactic was to swamp us with human waves. They were very courageous, and so, many died."[24]

It was in these tough hill battles of February and March that the Patricias got their real-life experiences in battle and acquired the confidence that if properly dug in, and given enough ammunition, they could probably always hold their own against the Chinese. It was this confidence in each other, more a sense of being self-assured than being smug, that accounts for their certainty at Kapyong that they could outfight anyone.

Wilfred Harold Olson/Department of National Defence/Library and Archives Canada, PA-171228.

Infantrymen of 2 PPCLI move in single file across rice paddies as they advance on enemy positions across the valley in March, a month before Kapyong. The soldier second from left has his Lee-Enfield rifle wrapped in protective burlap against the mud and damp weather.

But there's a world of difference between defending, as they would be at Kapyong, and attacking, as they were now. As a rule of thumb, a three-to-one ratio is needed to go on the attack; so it would take three hundred men, for example, to attack one hundred Chinese. At Kapyong the Patricias had the advantages of the defence. But not here and not now. Now, in March, those advantages lay with the Chinese, who were also experts and camouflage and concealment.

The most famous example of the classic defence is the pass at Thermopylae in which a handful of Spartans held off thousands of Persians — although it is often conveniently forgotten that the attacking Persians ultimately won, albeit through treachery. But, generally, putting money on the defence is the way to bet. History tends to forget the successful defenses and remembers mostly the disasters: Hastings, the Alamo, the Little Bighorn, Quebec, Batoche, Normandy, and Dien Bien Phu in Vietnam are other famous case studies of the defence going under.

However, in theory the Chinese, with their limitless supplies of manpower, would almost always have the edge in both attack and defence, which was a matter of great concern to the Americans and accounts for their love affair with massive artillery barrages and overwhelming air support to even the odds. They could not afford to get bogged down in a war which degenerated simply into a man-to-man slugging match with the Chinese. America and the rest of the U.N. forces were technology-rich and wanted to fight a war of planes, bombs, and shells. China was technology-poor, but peasant-rich, and preferred to throw mountains of men with rifles and grenades at their opponents and swarm them. That's how the Chinese had fought their civil war against each other. General Douglas MacArthur warned against becoming sucked like quicksand into "a land war in Asia," although it was an insight he developed after Korea, not during it.

But in the late winter of 1951, the shape of Canada's war against the Chinese was still of war of movement, attacking them, forcing them off their positions, and then back northwards. It was literally an uphill battle.

On March 4, General Matthew Ridgway, the overall commander in Korea, visited 2 PPCLI headquarters. Clearly something was up. On the 7th, a new U.N. offensive, "Operation Ripper," was launched to push across the 38th parallel, the so-called Kansas Line, the original boundary between the two Koreas.

After Hills 444 and 419 came Hill 532.

No one had ever heard of it. And except for those who fought there, it would soon vanish from history as the years went by. It was an awful place. It would be the worst day so far.

The men are up at three o'clock that morning, with the luxury of hot water for shaving. They were given a hot breakfast. It would be a busy day.

The paymaster was there. The men were able to make appropriate arrangements, in case of death. There would be surely be men killed before the day was done. Two padres held services for those wishing to attend.

The attack started about six o'clock a.m. By midday, snow began coming down in huge flakes that gave the hillsides an unreal, other-worldly beauty. On a neighbouring hill, Australians got pinned down barely a third of the way up.

An American forward artillery observer attached to the Patricias was celebrating his nineteenth birthday. The Canadians sang him a round of "Happy Birthday."

Like gladiators preparing to enter the Colosseum, the men girded themselves with bandoliers of ammunition, grenades, and the extra ammo they carried for the machine gunners.

Lieutenant Rod Middleton packed sixty-four rounds for his Browning 9mm pistol. He also carried a rifle so Chinese snipers would be less likely to single him out as an officer.

On the next hill, the Australians were meeting heavy opposition. The Patricias were starting to have problems of their own.

D Company went straight up the steep slope of the hill. A Company swung to the left and then north, also up the hill. After about forty-five minutes, having passed through a deserted village, D came under fire from well-hidden machine guns. Two men were hit and went down. They were in 10 Platoon, commanded by Mike Levy. There was a firefight for about twenty minutes, and then Levy's men inched forward again, trying to get to the cover of some brush. Middleton's platoon evacuated Levy's wounded and then advanced over frozen rice paddies. They assumed Levy's men were just to their front, but could see no sign of them. Where was Levy? As the Company moved into the open, out of the shrub, machine gun fire caught them from both sides. Middleton's men instantly returned fire. A Chinese soldier popped out of his hole and started running, only to be picked off and have his body tumble down the hill.

"The enemy begins to mortar us," said Middleton. "I order the men to dig in. Off to my left I see the US mortar radioman advancing up the hill, alone, in the open, unaware of the enemy. We try to warn him. In a flash a Chinese soldier popped up from his hole and with his burp gun, cuts him to shreds."[25]

Photo by Hub Gray.

Lieutenant Mike Levy of 10 Platoon in foreground, with beret and paratrooper wings, returning from a patrol chasing communist guerrillas, shortly before Kapyong. The men are descending a 4,000 foot mountain while in winter gear in eighty degree Fahrenheit weather. Levy was a natural leader whose bravery was matched only by his modesty.

With the American mortar radioman gone, the link with the mortar crews themselves was also gone. The mortar spotter, the man with the attacking troops who would be the person to direct the mortar crews where to place their fire, had no way to communicate. He joined in with the Patricias as an infantryman.

At this point Levy and his men emerged. They'd made a navigation error and had gotten lost, climbing and descending a saddle between two hills in the wrong direction, and plodded through the snow for four hours. They were exhausted. Nonetheless, the Company commander ordered Levy's men to join in a new attack with the others. Middleton offered to lead the advance and let Levy be in reserve. By 9:30 D Company had taken three casualties. By 1:30 in the afternoon, a further seven, including one killed.

The terrain was so steep, rough, and wild it was impossible for the Company to concentrate its attack on individual positions, so the large

Company assault broke down into small, individual actions by platoons, or even sections of ten men, with lone riflemen shooting at whatever they could spot. Hill 532 was a case study of the Canadians being hopelessly outgunned with their bolt-action rifles while the Chinese blazed away with their automatic weapons. No one could leapfrog forward, and the attack stalled because the Patricias could not generate enough firepower to provide covering fire to force the Chinese to keep their heads down.

American tanks bravely moved in and gave supporting fire, but the men still remained pinned down. A Company dug in part way up the hill. It was coming under increasingly heavy fire and paths to the top were being blocked by huge rocks and boulders. Their assault stalled. Men were being hit all the way up.

For John Bishop in A Company, the scene they discovered where they were prepared to tough it out for the night was one of carnage and horror.

> The Chinese had captured the position from the Americans only a few days before, they they'd left the corpses of GIs strewn about like animal carcasses. Perhaps I was becoming inured to death because strange to say, after the first shock, it was not the sight of this charnel house that bothered me as much as the social injustice manifested there. As in my last encounter with mass death, all the dead were black soldiers. This time, however, the exception was a young and frail white 2nd Lieutenant, presumably the commander, with a neat hole from a small caliber bullet between his eyes. [Bishop does not say so, but the implication is that a small-calibre bullet would be from a pistol, not a rifle, and the man had been executed.]
>
> As Canadian boys most of us were repelled by the US Army's policy that denied the full humanity to these Afro-Americans who'd been good enough to die for their country, but not good enough to fight for it as equals.[26]

Darkness closed in and there was no time to tend to the dead. There was scarcely time for his ten man section to beef up their defenses and sight in their shooting positions. Bishop decided to settle in for the night in a large slit trench he inherited from the departed Chinese.

From here he calculated how he could best command his section.

"I groped around in the litter left in it and made a place to lie down. The trench was uncomfortable. I hadn't had a chance to look at it in daylight, let alone clean it up. I was lying on top of a jumble of military kit — a pack, what I thought was a bed roll which served as my pillow, a rifle and other odds and ends. I drifted into a fitful doze on my uneven bed with anonymous things sticking into me."[27]

Bishop captures the horror of infantry warfare with the graphic skill of a novelist — except this was real life.

He awoke in the morning of the 8th, literally looking death in the face.

> I opened my eyes to see a pair of bloodshot eyes staring back at me. I was resting on my cheek, none-to-nose with another face almost touching mine. Not yet fully awake I tried to figure out where I was … then, coming to with a jolt, I discovered I'd slept with a dead Chinese soldier as my trench mate. I bolted up right and had a look at my bed.
>
> What I thought was my bedroll, I'd used as a pillow, turned out to be the thigh of a dismembered limb still wearing the pant leg and boot of an American GI. Thankfully the freezing cold preserved the dead flesh.[28]

For years afterward, Bishop would awake with a start staring into those bloodshot eyes.

Over at D Company, they now attacked upward with fixed bayonets, through snow six inches deep. The ground was wet and slippery. As they began to take fire from three sides, the assault started to become disorganized and confused. What little momentum there was was lost.

The battalion's War Diary in its dry, mechanical style, still gives a whiff of what it must have been like:

> By 14:10 hours A Company was encountering stiff enemy resistance.... at 14:00 hours, D company began

its final attack for the day and this time managed to get up on the first ridge held by the Chinese, but this ridge was in turn dominated by an even more strongly held position about 100 yards further on. By this time D Company had become somewhat disorganized due to the intense fire it was receiving from three sides and had had heavy casualties in the last assault.

The position was untenable and at 16:00 hours the CO (Stone) ordered D Company to pull back carefully. The company did so under heavy small arms fire and the Chinese reoccupied their last position making it impossible to recover the bodies of the men killed in the last attack.[29]

The War Diary provides the big picture, perhaps. But it is somehow detached, formal, and stilted. "Fire was received from three sides" has a distant, clerk-like ring to what must have been a terrifying experience in which a flurry of bullets smash their way into human forms as gasping men with their hearts pounding like jackhammers scramble for cover.

The gruesome detail and the smell, sounds, and chaos of actual close-quarter infantry combat come not from official reports written later in a calmer moment, but from the men doing the actual fighting. Read on, and sense what it was like to be with Mike Levy as the Chinese were showering them with grenades. Suddenly, the unstoppable Mike Levy was stopped.

"I came across six or seven men, wounded or killed, lying fairly close together," he said later. "I stopped to pick up a rifle. I was holding it in front of my chest, checking the ammunition in the magazine. Either a bullet or a grenade fragment hit the rifle slamming it into my chest with a terrific force and knocking me out. I eventually careened down the hill for some distance."[30]

Ron Rushton, a corporal, takes over the attack. "As I neared the top of the first incline a chap comes towards me, he is wounded and falls down, but gets up and falls again, his eyes are glassy and there he dies … this is suicidal to keep going, we do not have enough men."[31]

Middleton, who was at the centre of the fighting through the entire action, reached the front enemy trench. His senior non-commissioned officer, Swede Larson, and two other men arrived and started handing out more hand grenades. Larson began to lob a grenade, but was hit in the shoulder mid-toss. Sergeant B.W. Holligan was fifteen feet away. He miraculously caught the grenade and flung it out of the way. He was wounded by its shrapnel. Another sergeant was wounded and went down.

Middleton fought on as his men fell around him. "I continued my advance against the enemy and come across Private Wylie, twice-wounded in the chest, I dress his wounds and apply morphine, he dies on the hill. Further along in the trench I kill one enemy. I turn to call for supporting fire from my platoon, but I find myself alone."[32]

The account of Middleton's face-to-face combat on Hill 532 is terrifying to read, even six decades later. As he struggled up the slope he almost bumped into a Chinese soldier emerging from his position.

> Armed with a captured American rifle, the Chinese soldier fired but missed. He attempted to fire again, but his rifle jammed. The Canadian raised his pistol to fire, but his mud-coated weapon would not work either. With less than 10 yards between them, both men struggled frantically to clear their weapons in a macabre race to the death. The young Canadian officer managed to bring his weapon back into action first. He recounted what happened next: "I was so frightened that I let go 10 rounds before I realized he was falling backward. I reloaded my magazine. To go forward up the trench, I had to crawl over him. There was not much evidence of his wounds, just a row of white puffs on the back of his quilted winter uniform where the bullets had come out. I will never forget that experience of crawling over a still warm body."[33]

For the neighbouring Australians on the flank, it was also a bad day. They, too, failed to take their hill.

Throughout the night, Patricias' medics, under fire, tried to retrieve bodies. To add to the misery, the Chinese lobbed more than 100 grenades down onto the dug-in Canadians in the darkness.

At five o'clock the next morning, 2 PPCLI was at it again, only to discover that sometime during the night the Chinese had quietly abandoned the hilltop and withdrawn in the mists. The Chinese had been facing setbacks on other sections of the front during Operation Ripper and while they were pulling back all along, it seemed they had been reluctant to give up these well-prepared positions that were the target of the Canadians and Australians without a fight. Strangely, the pullout seemed to have been conducted in haste and panic. The Chinese had left their well-built strongpoints intact and not destroyed, and the landscape was strewn with full ammunition crates ... and eighty-two dead Chinese.

The acting D Company commander, a captain, reported to Jim Stone that Levy had under-performed during the battle. Stone, who knew a thing or two about leadership, instead removed the company commander from combat. Many of the troops felt the captain's plan for a frontal attack up a steep slope was hopeless from the start. Levy was left in command of his platoon.

A week after the battle for Hill 532, John Bishop was promoted to corporal and was slowly deciding he wanted, despite everything that happened this day, to make the Army his career, unlike most of his fellow volunteers in the battalion. Bishop stayed in for thirty-six years and retired with the rank of lieutenant-colonel.

Sergeant Holligan, who caught the loose grenade in mid-flight and was wounded tossing it free, had a habit of being heroic. Six years later during a jump, he rescued a paratrooper whose parachute got entangled outside the rear exit of his plane. Holligan risked his life (again) to save the soldier and was awarded the George Medal. It was presented by the Queen.

Len Barton, a private in the much-mauled D Company, was shot early in the assault. At almost the same time his platoon commander and several other men were also hit. A stunned Barton examined his wound, trying to decide what to do next, when he realized almost everyone else was down. Incredibly, he stood up, with bullets whizzing all around, and yelled at those still uninjured to follow him. He was hit several more times, but the rest of the men plunged forward, reacting to his leadership. Barton was awarded the Military Medal, the first Canadian to be decorated in Korea.

For the Patricias, Hill 532 had been a valiant, but chaotic and messy, affair. The day's fighting ended with seven dead Patricias and thirty-seven wounded, mostly from D Company. That's almost as many killed, and in fact more wounded, than at Kapyong. And who remembers Hill 532?

The neighbouring Australians had twelve killed and twenty-four wounded.

Overall, this was turning into a bloody enterprise. After three gruesome weeks of tough fighting in the mountains and hills, the Patricias had fourteen dead and forty-three wounded. In addition, eighty-six "non battle" casualties had been shipped off home. They were either anti-social misfits from the start, or men who psychologically could not cope with combat. Stone referred to these men as "scruff," and simply wanted to be rid of them, although some of the brass back in Canada felt the solution was to salvage and retrain the men. The problem solved itself. By the end of March, with the misfits gone, non-battle casualties dropped to a trickle and "real" casualties were filled by replacements.

It is lonely being a replacement in any army. These men were outsiders, artificially inserted into a tightly bonded group who'd trained together, fought together, and shared great dangers and many sorrows. The replacements knew no one and no one knew them or felt any particular attachment. If he were injured under fire, just maybe someone would risk it and try to help him, but maybe not. Soldiers will risk their lives for men they've fought alongside, but weren't likely to do so for a nameless stranger. The brutal reality was that to seasoned troops, a replacement's life simply was not worth as much as a veteran's. In fact, an inexperienced outsider was someone who could contribute nothing to the security of the group and was a downright liability.

Don Hibbs, ever the foxhole philosopher, gets right to the point: "If a new replacement arrives, we say 'So! You're the new recruit!' He'd be about to tell me his name and I'd say 'Don't tell me your name! If you're still with us next week and you're still alive, tell me then.'"[34]

After Hill 532, the exhausted Patricias pushed northward for five more days, pursuing the retreating Chinese but without making contact. For most there are only memories of hiking, digging, and clambering over hillsides, covering three or four miles each day, going

mostly upward. The weather was slowly warming and the snow melt-
ing. On March 15, they were finally taken out of the line to rest and
re-fit.

Despite the battering his battalion had been through, Jim Stone,
who had extremely high standards, gave his men good marks. First, he
was critical of their lack of care for their weapons; a curious observation
because every infantryman would know that his life depends on a clean
and oiled rifle, which would be his dearest possession.

Stone then continued on a more upbeat note: "Troops here are fit,
morale high, show lots of guts in close contact," he wrote. " ... Lack
of comfort which is general in this theatre is being compensated with
troops' own ingenuity covering weapons slits etc.... troops are well led
and the aggressiveness they display in attack under difficult circumstances is great credit to their officers."[35]

His men attack, he went on, "with Bren, rifle, bayonet and grenades,
usually from very close range. The climbs to the assault lines are most
fatiguing and it's a great credit to the troops that they show such great
determination in going in ... the men themselves are a great credit to
Canada and to their Battalion."[36]

He yet again stressed that the place to spot and weed out misfits was
back at basic training depots in Canada, not over here on the battlefield.

Stone also noted the rigours of the rough Korean landscape were hard
on gear. The men's clothes and boots wore out quickly, and American
boots were far superior, which even the humblest private could have told
him weeks earlier.

And he strangely and stubbornly stood by the Lee-Enfield bolt-
action rifle which clearly was from another era. With modifications, the
Lee-Enfield had been used by infantry since the Boer War. American
semi-automatic rifles were prone to malfunction in the dirt and frost of
Korea, he said, claiming soldiers who'd tried the U.S. Garand rifle eventually discarded them and went back to their Lee-Enfields. It's hard to
know how Stone came by this curious information.

Stone did not waste time while in reserve. He had a strong belief that
somewhere within his lowliest soldiers there could be great commanders, and like Napoleon, he sensed that in every corporal there could be a
future field marshal. Stone's own career was such a story. He established

training courses to train a new generation of future non-commissioned officers, such as sergeants. When the shooting starts, and combat is at close range and personal, it is the sergeants and corporals, not the generals, who actually direct the flow of battle and lead the men. An army can survive its foolish generals so long as its sergeants and corporals know their stuff.

No one was going to put on weight while in the rest area. Stone had a passion for realistic training in tactics and weaponry under combat conditions. The more "real" the training, the less of a surprise actual combat would be.

He also knew how to motivate his troops. While resting up, he made sure they had worn-out gear and clothing replaced, and saw to it they had regular mail, hot water, hot meals, and beer.

He authorized a celebration on the 17th, the birthday of Princess Patricia, after whom the Patricias were named. It looked like it would be a grand day and a thoughtful gesture from the commander. There was a band, a banquet, a huge bonfire, and a sing-along. Sadly, there was also some homemade booze.

In Stone's account: "When I awoke the next morning, I was immediately informed that there had been a great tragedy. There were four men dead, two blind and several others having their stomachs pumped out. They got into the canned heat (methanol) and had been mixing it with fruit juice and drinking the stuff after the party was over. There was really no person to blame. The whole thing was stupid and tragic. A few of the misfits who hadn't been weeded out perhaps. Today, there are probably two blind men somewhere in Canada who can trace their blindness back to that night."[37]

Ever the man to drive home a practical point, Stone paraded his troops in front of the bodies of the dead soldiers and lectured them on the consequences of stupidity. Everyone got the message. There is not a hint of this sad incident in the official history.

Canada's official history is curiously silent on several facets of the Korean War, such as the strange case of the mass murder of Chinese soldiers. In an account of a conflict spanning three years, involving millions of soldiers from many countries, certain value judgments enter into selecting what to include and what to drop, yet it is still odd that something as eerie as this tale would not make into the official record. It was mass murder. Canadians discovered it, but who were the killers? Why isn't it written down somewhere in some faded army file or dusty folder. Or was it in fact noted, but is long since lost in some ancient Department of Defence warehouse somewhere, mis-catalogued and unmissed?

This incident happened after Kapyong, but the exclusion of such a weird event raises questions of what else happened during the war that was dropped from the record — and for what reason.

These events occurred in May 1951, about two weeks after Kapyong. The Chinese had taken a brutal beating and had broken off contact. Prior to launching an offensive The Commonwealth Brigade, of which the Patricias were a part, were mounting patrols to scout out the land ahead. Sometimes there were skirmishes; sometimes not. On May 14, 12 Platoon (of D Company, which always seemed to be where things were going to happen) were patrolling near the small rail stop called Gumcochyi. It was a scorching day, about 85 degrees Fahrenheit, although the men were still in their winter clothing. Everyone had rolled up their shirtsleeves. As a special treat, they were not carrying field rations, but instead had a couple of sandwiches and an unbelievable treasure: an apple. If it only weren't for the war, it would have been a lovely day's walk in the sun.

Hub Gray, whose machine guns had saved headquarters at Kapyong, was leading the so-far uneventful patrol.

They spotted an enemy formation of some type about a kilometre ahead. Gray examined them through his binoculars. Nothing moved. It was very eerie. His men warily moved forward, suspecting they might have been heading into an ambush.

"It is so quiet our nerves are on edge anticipating at any moment a sudden burst of fire," Gray writes later. "After a cautious and tense ten-minute advance we come upon the enemy formation, comprising two officers, three NCOs, and 51 soldiers, 56 in all."[38]

All were dead. But that wasn't the half of it.

They were equipped with quality high-power binoculars, burp guns, machine guns, grenades, and a mortar. Usually the Chinese were short of weapons. But not these Chinese. And they weren't dressed in the normal green uniforms, but in some kind of formal summer dress uniform with brass buttons.

PPCLI Museum and Archives. Photo by Hub Gray.

12 Platoon, D Company, 2 PPCLI.

"They are all sitting on their haunches, torso bolt upright, uniformly at attention, as though they are seated in formation," writes Gray. "How the hell did these men die? What and who snuffed out their lives, and why are they positioned here, appearing like chessmen?"[39]

It was like a scene from a cheap Hollywood horror movie. They had no bullet holes or any other type of wound.

A Patricia tugged at a pair of binoculars resting on the chest of one of the dead men. They broke free, but part of the man's skin went with them, leaving a gaping hole almost ten inches across and a "black mass" poured out of the cavity. Inside, the body is was empty shell, the innards having been totally consumed.

Some of the soldiers vomited. Others moved away.

Gray suspected the dead Chinese had been the victims of some form of chemical or biological attack. His men were uneasy, fearing they may be contaminated with something themselves, wondering if they would be next. They quickly returned to their base and Gray wrote up a report for his company commander. He handed it in.

He expected to be told to lead a patrol back to the grim site the next day, but no such order was ever given. He heard nothing more about it.

Years of sleuthing have brought Gray no closer to finding answers. There's no record of anyone else returning to the scene to investigate; no sign of what eventually happened to the bodies; no clues as to which side killed the men because the site had been in the control of both sides at the time. Gray's personal hunch is that the massacre was the handiwork of the Russians, but what were they up to? Was it chemicals or germs? It certainly wasn't gunfire. Who were these men, anyway, with their unusual uniforms? And other patrols must have stumbled across the scene; where are their reports?

In later years, to ensure that the story would not be lost to history and that its retelling would not rely solely on his memory and word alone, Gray tracked down some of the men on his patrol that day and had them sign corroborating statements of what they'd all seen.

James Waddiandy, a lance corporal at the time, said: "I remember clearly … enemy soldiers all in three lines … like a platoon … all dead. They were in a sort of sitting position, rigidly upright, all of them. It was not natural."[40]

Private George Nestor well remembers: "… found a whole platoon of enemy soldiers, dead in some kind of mass formation. The information caused one hell of a buzz amongst us because of the queer way in which they all died at one time, on their knees, sitting on their haunches … we expected there would be another patrol to investigate the whole thing, but nothing happened."[41]

Private Neil Neufeld: "The enemy troops were in line like an oversized platoon. All dead, sitting upright. Bloody peculiar, I thought."[42]

The mystery of the dead Chinese remains unsolved. No one has any idea what happened near the abandoned Gumcochyi rail station, why it happened, or who did it.

Piled atop those enigmas is yet another final one: even though Gray wrote a full official report the same day for his commander, today in the 2 PPCLI War Diary where the regiment's archives are kept in Calgary, there is no trace of the incident to be found. The official history is also silent. Often, so much of the real story of wars comes from the mouths of ordinary soldiers who fought them, and not from governments and armies and generals.

Coming out of a rest and refit period after the Hill 532 battles, the Patricias returned to combat, pursuing the retreating Chinese, pushing across the 38th parallel by early April into what is technically North Korea.

Family and sweethearts back home were anxious, as they had been since armies were going at it with axes and swords. This nasty Korean business was turning out to be far removed from the occupation duty they assumed their boys were heading into what seemed like millions of years ago last December when they boarded the *Martinez*. Murray Edwards's sister, Margaret, sent her brother a prayer: "On the battle-fields of Korea our men are fighting still … Dear God, won't you lend a hand as you've done before since the world began. I've a brother now fighting there. We pray he's safely kept within your care. Please God, watch over him as he goes to fight."[43]

Edwards survived the war.

As the Patricias chased their foe further and further north, the Chinese had all the advantages of defence, and used small groups of men to harass and hinder much larger pursuing forces. In attacks on Hills 826 and 795, supported by plenty of artillery, D Company (again) was in the thick of it, as was 10 Platoon's Mike Levy, who the War Diary says attacks with great spirit, before being ordered by Jim Stone to call it off. They'd suffered five wounded. Finally, on the morning of the 15th, the Chinese withdrew and the Canadians occupied the heights.

It was a frustrating style of war to fight for soldiers with such great dash, élan, and aggressiveness. Aside from the exhilaration of combat, it was difficult for the troops to calculate what all this meant, if anything. If they took a hill, fine, they had the satisfaction of a successful mission. If they didn't, then the Chinese held a hill in the middle of nowhere, and who cared? None of this seemed to be affecting the destiny of nations, exactly. But they had come to Korea to fight, and they were getting what they had come for. There was more to come.

On April 18, they were taken out of the line and replaced by South Korean troops. The Patricias went into a rest zone a few miles from a nothing little village. It was Kapyong.

The Chinese armies were disengaging from the front, such as it was, following their strategy of withdrawing in the face of strength, and re-grouping for a decisive engagement. On the night of the 22nd, the Chinese opened their new offensive. The plan was to force a hole in the front, charge through the gap, and make for Seoul or wherever fortune presented a promising opportunity.

The first blow fell on the hapless ROK (Republic of Korea) 6th Division. By about eight o'clock, they had smashed into the South Koreans, just north of Kapyong. The Chinese had found the weakest point in the line. By eleven o'clock the South Korean commander had lost contact with his army and his troops were fleeing their posts, abandoning their weapons, and equipment. The Patricias and the rest of the commonwealth division were no longer in reserve. They were back in the war.

That same afternoon, some Canadian officers were visiting a nearby New Zealand artillery base that was hosting a goodbye party for some British troops. In an offhanded way they noticed refugees began streaming by. The phone rang. The message: "A bit of a sticky wicket is developing at the front."[44]

The party was over. Everyone raced back to their units.

Stone had just returned to his Battalion, just recovered from smallpox he probably caught in an old abandoned Korean farm a month earlier.

Sergeant Alex Sim noticed a flurry of meetings: "Suddenly senior NCOs and officers were gathering. I thought 'Oh Oh!' For some strange reason in the back of my mind a very small light flickered and I thought: *something is wrong*. Then the light went on. I don't know why I did it but I did. I started issuing ammunition and grenades to my troops. Later I was told the front had collapsed and were moving up to plug holes."[45]

The Kapyong area is at the intersection of north-south and east-west roads. To anyone wanting to break into the South, Kapyong would be a front door. If you wanted to lock that door, you had to control Kapyong. Two streams met at Kapyong, forming a *Y*-shaped depression between two steep hills. The Chinese would come along the valley floor between those hills. Control those two hills: you control the valley.

The right hill, Hill 504, was assigned to the 3RAR, the Third Battalion of the Royal Australian Regiment, and an American tank unit, the 72nd Heavy Tank Battalion. They were to dig in on the north slopes. Their time at Kapyong would be both heroic and terrible.

A mile or so to the west, on their hill, would be the Patricias. The men atop these two hills had no protection on either side and were highly vulnerable to flanking attacks in which they could be surrounded.

It's the kind of question they'd put to young officers in a classroom exercise: you're surrounded. Now what?

But this was no classroom.

CHAPTER 5

THE BATTLE BEGINS:
"LET THE BASTARDS COME!"

T echnically, it was just a notation on a map: Hill 677, indicating its elevation in metres above sea level. Hardly a name to die for.

About twenty-five miles northeast of Seoul, it wasn't so much a hill as a series of interconnecting ridges. Separating the ridges were steep sides. Their very steepness was a lifesaver.

But those steep ridges also presented a dilemma for the Canadians in planning a traditional defence. Ideally, a battalion of around 800 men is supposed to be able to defend itself, with the companies within it supporting each other. But the unevenness of the terrain forced the Patricias to break up into smaller groups, the companies, which, in most cases, meant they could not even see each other even in daylight, let alone support each other.

Each company would have to fight its own fight, depending only on the platoons within those companies for mutual support. But there would be moments in the battle to come when even platoons, and sometimes even sections of ten men, would be fighting on their own. Indeed, there were instances of two men in a foxhole fighting their own little war, all alone against the Chinese.

Custer at the Battle of Little Bighorn is the nightmare scenario that comes to mind when contemplating what can happen when units are broken down into smaller pieces and can't come to each other's aid when an emergency arrives at full gallop. This is a sure-fire recipe for becoming surrounded and cut off. Despite about 250 cavalrymen against perhaps 3,000 Lakota and Cheyenne, the annihilation of the 7th Cavalry was not axiomatic. There were many instances of outnumbered cavalry surviving battles on the Plains, even when isolated and cut off. But to pull it off, they had to remain together and fight as a solid unit. At Little Bighorn, Custer divided his troops into separate columns. They were attacked piecemeal in a string of battles scattered across a series of little hilltops and ravines. They were isolated and then picked off one-by-one. Other troops only a few miles off were too far removed to come to their rescue, or weren't even aware of the crisis. None of the scattered cavalrymen with Custer survived. Other 7th Cavalry columns who stuck together did. This was the tactical question facing Jim Stone at Kapyong: how to form an effective defence even though he was forced to fight his battle piecemeal. It's not known if Stone was aware of the Canadian dimension to Custer's Last Stand, but he surely knew of Custer's fate. About forty of the cavalrymen at the Little Bighorn were Canadians (and one Newfoundlander) who'd gone down to the U.S. to join the Union Army. Many were Civil War veterans who'd stayed on. One was Lieutenant William Cooke, who was Custer's adjutant, and who scribbled the last desperate message to other units as they galloped into the fight, asking for more ammo. Cooke died along with everyone else and is now buried in his hometown, Hamilton, Ontario.

But Stone was convinced he could avoid being "Custerized" if, despite the numbers involved and the rough terrain that broke up so much of the cohesion of his force, he could come up with a solid plan and had solid troops. He was right on both counts. Stone was no dreamer who thought hoping for the best would do the trick. He had the best tactical mind Canada ever produced. And he was an utter realist without an ounce of sentimentality who coolly calculated the odds, and concluded he could pull it off.

You can still visit Kapyong and see what Jim Stone saw. A tourist today could drive by and not give the place a moment's thought, except to wonder why any of it was worth dying for. Not much has changed in the neighbourhood in the last six decades. Now it's quiet, lush, and pretty, unlike in April 1951, when the sounds of combat were just over the horizon, the hillside was barren except for straggly bush, and the ground had been scooped out by shellfire. There's still no urban sprawl

Directorate of History and Heritage, 681.019 (D2).

Looking due east from the top of Kapyong (Hill 677), towards the valley the main Chinese forces came through. In the right background is Hill 504 the Australians held until forced off.

extending out from the little town. Where the steep slopes of the hill before had only shattered tree stumps and scorched shrubs, now there are dense growths of rowan, catkin, pine trees, and rhododendrons. The valley below is lush with rice paddies and vegetables. And near the foot of the hill is a lovingly-tended memorial. Few visiting veterans of the battle, now in their eighties, can make their way right to the top any longer. If they did, only the sharp-eyed could just barely spot the last traces of overgrown slit trenches and fox holes. No one calls this place Hill 677. This is Kapyong. This was where the Patricias would make their stand.

Jim Stone arrived with some of his staff, but ahead of his troops, for reconnaissance. As he proved in the mountain fighting in Italy, he had a brilliant eye for ground and a knack for "reading" the terrain spreading out before him, much as an architect would work with his plans for a skyscraper.

Stone was imagining in his mind's eye where to place his troops, how could they be best protected, how they could communicate with each other, if they could support each other when the going got rough, were there blind spots, and where the enemy could slip by and pounce. The German Field Marshall, Erwin Rommel, the famed Desert Fox, had a gift that his admirers called *Fingerspitzegefühl*, meaning a sort of sixth sense feeling in your fingertips. Stone had it, too.

He went out in front, where the Chinese were going to come up at him, from the north side of the hill. He wanted to see what the enemy would see; to plan how he would have attacked his own position. Stone firmly believed that time spent on reconnaissance was never wasted.

This is how he later described what he saw and how his mind was working as he approached the fight of his life:

> I took forward a large reconnaissance party of company commanders, gunner rep [representative], mortar rep, and the battalion MMG and mortar platoon commanders. We were able to look at the feature from the enemy side, which gave us a good idea of probable attack approaches. Therefore, I was able to select the vital ground which had to be defended to deny the approaches to the enemy.
>
> Hill 677 is about a mile and a half across, gullied, wooded and impossible to defend in the classic manner of deploying companies to support each other. Each company had to develop its own individual defended locality, the platoons being mutually supporting. The gaps between the companies would have to be covered, to some extent, by defensive fire tasks of the MMGs, the battalion 81mm mortars, the US mortar company and the New Zealand 25-pounder regiment.[1]

Stone liked to fight his battles from the hilltops, making the enemy do most of the work, climbing up at you, lugging his ammunition and weapons with him, loads that would grow heavier with each tired step. It was a defensive style. And while defence doesn't win wars, it can save the day until there's a better tomorrow. When vastly outnumbered, as the Canadians would be, the defence was by far the best tactical choice.

Stone calculated that if his companies could not cover neighbouring companies, each individual company could hopefully defend itself. But they would be on utterly their own. It was not so much a gamble as a calculated risk. It certainly was not the defensive posture of choice, but it was the best and the wisest plan Stone could devise given the shrinking time and resources he had on hand. It was an improvised solution. This was the type of initiative at which Stone excelled and which he expected in turn from his soldiers, echoing the old military adage "when it's time to go, you go with what you've got."

The gaps between companies would have to be covered somehow by the battalion's own machine guns and mortar units, which would be placed near Stone's command post roughly in the centre of the Canadian position. The companies were spaced apart in an arc separated by roughly 330 yards, and their isolation because of those intervening ravines reinforced the sensation that each was on its own and isolated. Adding to the tension was the increasingly likelihood that the fighting, when it came, would probably be close-up.

Working in their favour, bush and shrubbery in front of many positions had been crushed flat by the previous winter's heavy snow, and that, combined with the rugged terrain, meant the approach routes would give the enemy little cover and they'd have to make their move over open ground. And the very steepness of the slopes would force the attackers to come not head on, but at an angle. It was hoped support would be available from an American mortar and New Zealand artillery units.

Three miles to the east on a smaller hill would be an Australian unit, the 3rd Battalion Royal Australian Regiment (RAR) and the American 72nd Heavy Tank Battalion.

Late on the afternoon on the 23rd, the Patricias began moving into their positions.

This is how Stone would deploy his forces to fight his battle: Imagine Kapyong roughly as a fat boomerang, arcing northward. Charlie company was facing due north at about twelve o'clock; Able Company just to the right and slightly south; Baker Company still further to the south of A Company; Dog Company was dangerously isolated on the extreme left, at about the three o'clock position; and B and D Companies were the ones to follow most closely.

Commanding 10 Platoon in D Company was young Mike Levy, a charismatic figure with a natural flair for combat and a character straight out of a war novel.

Born in India, the son of a British geologist, Levy grew up in Shanghai, was captured by the Japanese, and interned along with his family in the infamous Lungwha Civil Assembly Camp (depicted in the Steven Spielberg movie *Empire of the Sun*). Along with four others he escaped, and over the next two and a half months, aided by guerrillas, made his way on foot 1,988 miles across occupied China. Still only eighteen years old, he linked up with American Army Air Force units who flew him over the Himalayas to India. There, Levy then joined the Special Operations Executive (SOE), the British sabotage-espionage group skilled in blowing things up, and he fought behind the lines as a guerrilla. He started as a second lieutenant, was promoted to lieutenant and then to captain. He was now only twenty. Levy and his team were parachuted into Malaya where he was "mentioned in dispatches," a recognition of bravery that dates from Caesar's time. After the Japanese defeat he stayed on in Malaya to fight a communist insurgency. In a British army personnel report he was described as, "A young chap with previous experience of guerrillas ... full of guts and really is at his happiest when Japs or puppets were reported in the vicinity."[2]

Hundreds of Chinese Canadians volunteered to serve in Asia with the SOE. For many it was an affirmation of their patriotism, despite the racial discrimination they'd suffered at home. They'd hoped at war's end their bravery would earn them acceptance of complete equality. They were mostly teenagers, and their harrowing story of valour is little known in Canada today.

Mike Levy, who spoke a Chinese dialect, served alongside these remarkable soldiers, and from them learned about Canada. This prompted him to immigrate to Canada after the war, where he went into the restaurant business in Vancouver. It was not to his taste. A warrior at heart, he joined the special force in 1950 to fight in Korea. Levy's heroism at Kapyong was to play a pivotal part at a desperate moment in the battle. Levy was a perfect example of the right man at the right place whose hour had come. However, his valour was mysteriously to go unrecognized for more than a half a century, until brought to light by the investigative journalism of Hub Gray, who himself also played a distinguished role in the battle.

Directorate of History and Heritage, 681.019 (D2).

Looking WSW at the valley through which the Chinese attacked Colonel Stone's headquarters on the night of April 24, 1951.

Stone's headquarters was in the centre of the battalion, his soldiers positioned in a semi-circle around him, protected on his south only by a few machine guns and mortars. When the fighting began, B and D companies, and the mortar men and machine gunners, would be at the centre of the onslaught.

There was an army photographer assigned to the battalion, but he was away on leave in Japan at the time of Kapyong, which happened unexpectedly, so the cameraman missed the opportunity of a lifetime. A few of the soldiers had small film cameras of their own, bulky and primitive by today's standards, but these men became too busy shooting their rifles to bother with shooting pictures. Hence, there are no photographs of the actual fighting at Kapyong. One Patricia, Corporal Mike Melnechuck from Kamloops, shot a fifteen-minute colour "home movie" that included scenes from the battle, sent it home to Kodak in Canada for processing, and it was never seen again. Melnechuck, who died in 2010, shot much film during his time in Korea, but it has vanished without a trace.

Kapyong was but one in a series of targets the Chinese were preparing to annihilate in this latest offensive.

Three tragedies were about to unfold and they all had an immediate impact on what would eventually occur at Kapyong. The South Koreans, to the Patricias' north, were imploding. The Glosters, to the left, would soon be surrounded and in desperate fighting, destroyed as a fighting unit. Finally, the Australians to the right were swamped and averted the fate of the Glosters only, after much desperate fighting, by pulling out of their position.

It is too easy to underplay what the Patricias did at Kapyong and to assume that what they did was not that remarkable, until it is remembered what befell every one of their neighbours.

First on the Chinese "things-to-do" list were the South Koreans and British. About 19 miles to the west of the Patricias, early in the morning of April 23, about 30,000 Chinese crossed the Imjin River by night, the 1st Battalion of the Gloucestershire Regiment came under Chinese attack, the same time the South Koreans were being attacked north of Kapyong.

The British, although they'd been in position for a couple of weeks, had not built strong defensive positions. They had strung very little barbed wire and had laid few mines. They had not studied the river to see where fording was likely, and, as one officer said later, they just didn't seem to be in a serious defensive frame of mind. This was an extremely dangerous attitude, and was utterly at odds with the way Jim Stone would prepare for his battle.

Three British units were soon in fierce fighting as the Chinese swarmed across the river. By the afternoon of the next day, all were in serious trouble and the Chinese were in among them. But the Glosters's situation was truly dire. They were cut off.

The Glosters's commander, Lieutenant Colonel J.P. Cairne, was given permission to abandon the hill. But he'd been told a relief column was attempting to reach him, and rather than abandon his wounded, he decided to wait. As it turned out, the relief force couldn't make it.

Now the American-British language gap came into play, with dire consequences. The American divisional commander asked Cairne's boss, Brigadier Thomas Brodie, how his Glosters battalion was holding up. In other words, did the Glosters need help or not? Brodie said, with classic British understatement, that the situation the Glosters were in was "pretty sticky." The American misinterpreted this to mean things were serious, but the Glosters could hold out. And so no second relief column was sent. The Glosters were doomed.

Early on the 25th, with an ever-so-thin chance of survival still available, Brodie told the Americans that the Glosters could use some artillery support, but that essentially they were okay. In fact, as an effective fighting force, they were in their last moments. By 8:30 a.m. the last of the radio batteries died and the last link with the artillery, on whom they depended for survival, was severed.

Finally, on the night of the 24th, the Glosters were given permission to try to break out, but it was far too late. A handful, around forty, fought their way out, but the rest of the battalion was virtually annihilated. More than 700 men were killed or taken prisoner. The medical officer and padre volunteered to go into captivity with the men. Thirty-nine men died while POWs.

The commanding officer, Cairne, managed to evade capture for a day, but was eventually captured along with a small band of soldiers who were with him. Cairne received the Victoria Cross. Lieutenant Phillip Curtis, who had recently learnt of his wife's death and who died in a lone counter-attack on enemy machine guns, was also awarded the Victoria Cross, posthumously. Lieutenant Edward Waters, cited for heroism while a captive of the North Koreans, was awarded a George Cross, posthumously.

As the Canadians dug in to defend their hill just down the road, Gloster Hill was a grim example of what could lie in store. It reinforced their determination to tough it out together no matter what, rather than to try to break up into small units and make a run for it. The British soldiers had fought with great heroism and bravery, but the plan of the British defence was flawed and they had failed to communicate to the Americans how dire their situation was. There were recriminations later between British and American commanders. The U.S. high command let it be known they expected positions to be held as long as possible, which is not the same as fighting to the death for no good reason. It would be a fine line of judgement for a field commander to gauge the difference between the two. None of this would apply to the Patricias. There was no such confusion in the Canadian position. The Canadians and the American high command were literally speaking the same language and used the same slang and nuance. There was no confusion or "noise" in the system. Stone's deployment of his forces was a masterpiece of the defence. He was absolutely focused and knew the difference between a gamble and a calculated risk. He knew what his men were capable of, and while the fight would be a desperate one, it would not be a fight to the last bullet. Gloster Hill, he was certain, would not repeat itself atop Kapyong. There would be no last stand.

But there was another crisis in the making right on his doorstep. Around mid-afternoon, the road cutting through the valley in front of the Patricias, which was normally almost empty this time of day, was suddenly filling with people, some walking, many running, interspersed with military vehicles.

This was the second of three disasters. The first was the Gloster Hill debacle. Now it was the South Korean collapse.

These dusty swarms on the valley road were the remnants of the shattered South Korean 6th Division. The front line had come to the Patricias.

"There were huge numbers of people going past," remembers Mike Czuboka. "It was the ROKs and there were civilians retreating with them. We heard all these people going by and we hadn't the vaguest idea who they were. There could have been Chinese in with them. There were, in fact, Chinese mixed in. The Canadians couldn't afford to let them get close. If they did, some soldiers just opened fire."[3]

Captain Murray Edwards of Victoria, British Columbia, also remembers, "they all came streaming back in front of us. The Chinese were mixed in with them. It was a mixture of Koreans and Chinese."[4]

The sight of the fleeing South Korean troops angered some of the Canadians who'd come across the world to defend this place.

"I was stunned to see an unending line of ROK soldiers, walking in single file," says Corporal Rollie Lapointe, a trapper and hunter from La Pas, Manitoba. "We had not even begun to dig in. It reminds me of the photographs that I have seen of the Yukon, during the Gold Rush, of the miners hiking over the Chilkoot trail mountain pass. These men were armed and intent on going only in one direction. South! I shudder in disbelief at seeing our allies running away from the advancing enemy; they are a disorganized rabble! Leaving us to face their enemy to fight for their bloody country."[5]

Some South Korean officers began to shoot their soldiers in a vain attempt to restore order, re-assert their authority, and stop the stampede to the rear.

The Korean troops had not even spiked their abandoned artillery pieces to make them unusable. Their weapons could now be easily used by the Chinese. Also left behind as an unintended gift for the Chinese were ammunition, fuel, and trucks. The Korean division had simply disintegrated as a military unit.

Captain Owen Browne, the officer commanding A Company, was dug in the forward most position on Kapyong. He calculated (incorrectly, as it turned out) that his men would be the first to receive the full force of the Chinese assault. With a reporter's sense of graphic detail and mood, he captured the mayhem of the disaster unfolding in front of him.

> It was then, about mid-afternoon [April 23], that the rumour of the collapsing front acquired a meaning. From my arrival until then both the main Kap'yong Valley and the subsidiary valley cutting across the front had been empty of people. Then suddenly, down the road through the subsidiary valley came hordes of men, running, walking, interspersed with military vehicles — totally disorganized mobs. They were elements of the 6th ROK Division, which were supposed to be ten miles forward engaging the Chinese. But they were not engaging the Chinese. They were fleeing! I was witnessing a rout. The valley was filled with men. Some left the road and fled over the forward edges of "A" Company positions. Some killed themselves on the various booby traps we had laid, and that component of my defensive layout became worthless.
>
> I saw drivers of military vehicles run over their own men, wilfully. I saw owe man shoot the driver of a vehicle, pull him out to the ground, take over the vehicle and proceed. Between 15:30 and 18:00 hours all of A company speeded up its defensive preparations, and digging in as it watched, helpless to intervene, while approximately 4000-5000 troops fled in disorganized panic across and through the forward edges of our positions. But we knew then that we were no longer 10-12 miles behind the line; we were the front line.[6]

This is where the Chinese entered the valley to begin their assault on Kapyong and the Australian position, looking north.

The fall of the British Glosters was happening out of sight, at least, to the Patricias' west. But the South Korean implosion was right there in front of them.

Another disaster was at hand. About two miles to the east was the 3rd Royal Australian Regiment. Just after midnight, the Chinese swarmed the Australian positions on Hill 504. It was slightly lower than the Patricias' position (740 yards), which made it much tougher to defend. The Patricias' had a gallery seat to the drama about to unfold, and waited and watched.

Machine gunner Bill Chrysler had no doubts what was in store: "We knew they were coming because the South Koreans were on the run. The Aussies, well, we could look right at them and see them getting it. We knew we were going to get it next. A chill went through my spine."[7]

Sergeant Alex Sim learned an important lesson fast: "There were rumours that Chinese never attacked at night. We discovered that was a real myth. The Chinese frequently attacked at night, as a matter of fact, more often than not."[8]

He watched the Australian agony begin: "I could see the Aussies take a terrible beating. They were only about 1,000 yards to our right. I could make out figures moving about amid shell bursts."

At Stone's headquarters, Lance Corporal H.R. Crocker sat in a Jeep monitoring radio traffic with the rest of the Commonwealth force and American units who were trying to estimate the size of the various enemy forces and track their movement. For two hours Crocker plotted the points on a map. He realized the Patricias were now being encircled. Stone was called over, studied the map, and snapped: "Soldier, are you sure of those grid references?"

Crocker replied simply: "Yes Sir!"

Stone fingered the map some more, then said: "My God, we could be run over." He ordered the fuel cans removed from all vehicles, and had them placed on the ground with matches on top. If the enemy was about to swamp them, it would all be torched. Stone then said they were about two-and-a-half miles from friendly territory. If they were overrun, everyone would be on their own.[9]

During the night, the Australians in their trenches lost radio contact with their headquarters, then finally reported a pitched battle in which they and the Chinese were firing at point-blank range with Chinese troops swarming into the forward trenches and climbing onto American tanks helping to defend the hill.

PPCLI Captain Owen Browne, dug on the northern edge of Hill 677, eavesdropped on the nearby Australians' increasingly desperate wireless radio transmissions: "There was a 'mush' sound of a transmitting radio wave which is not carrying a voice. Someone was holding down the microphone switch, but was not speaking. And then I heard in a course whisper: 'There's about 200 of them now! About 600 yards away!'"

Browne then heard an interminable pause between each message. Finally: "'They've stopped and they seem to be forming up … there's more than 200. They are approaching. They are passing to the left of copse SHARK TAIL [a geographic feature to the Australian front]. They are about 400 yards away. DON'T FIRE … they're about 200 yards away. They've reached WHALEBONE. FIRE!!'"[10]

The Australians fended off a series of attacks, but eventually the sheer numbers of the Chinese and the indifference of their commanders to casualties made the difference.

By early evening the Australians were forced to make a fighting withdrawal. Sim saw it all: "I could see them start to abandon their position. There were explosions in the darkness as they destroyed the gas and ammo they couldn't carry."

Don Hibbs thought at the time: "Great. At least it's not us. But when they pulled out, I felt, *Now we're all alone.*"

The Australians lost thirty-one men killed and almost twice as many wounded. Three men were taken prisoner. It had been a heroic, but terrifying, night battle.

Jim Stone, seeing what had happened across the valley, adjusted one of his companies, B Company, moving it to cover his eastern flank where the Australians were getting a hammering. Such a shifting of some of his men ensured that Stone was now covering the side door of his position. The back door of his headquarters was protected by his mortar and heavy machine-gun crews. This minutiae of moving B Company to the eastern flank is no minor, arcane point of concern to armchair strategists. It turned out to be another of Stone's eerie insights into sensing the flow of battle on his real-life, three-dimensional chessboard. The Kapyong story is full of such small events and decisions that had enormous impact on the battle by affecting what did not happen. If this minor adjustment by riflemen from a single Company had not happened, the Patricias' eastern flank would have been unprotected and would have ultimately been swarmed. Stone felt that if he sensed this weak spot had been left unprotected, so, too, would the Chinese. The headquarters, and finally the hill itself, would then have been lost. Stone, with his intuitive tactical radar, sensed this peril and took steps to avert it by moving B Company.

Evening on the 24th set in. Nothing chills an infantryman more than the realization that he is surrounded, especially as night falls. Suddenly every innocent rock and every patch of shadow seems alive with menace. Even silence has an eerie noise to it. About 9:30 p.m. that night, reports started trickling in of enemy soldiers in their thousands massing in front of one of the platoon positions and circling around them in the darkness. This is where the army's poor choice of weapons for its troops on the line put the 700 Patricia infantrymen at a grave disadvantage for this kind of war.

Members of the 2 PPCLI steady themselves during mortar firing, about two months before Kapyong. Mortar crews like these were crucial in preventing Jim Stone's headquarters from being attacked from the rear and overrun.

The Patricias' prospects now looked dangerous indeed. The British to the west had fallen. The Koreans at their front collapsed. The Australians to the east were forced to abandon their trenches or go under.

Now it was the lonely Patricias' turn for the Chinese treatment.

"Night time is harrowing," remembers Lance Corporal Bill White of 10 Platoon, the most exposed platoon in the most exposed Company on the far left. "It's scary even if nothing is going on. Even a mouse or a rat or a snake crawling through the bush and breaking a twig would scare the hell out of you. We were ordered to have bayonets fixed. And they were fixed all the time."[11]

This is how the Chinese plan would unfold: first, B Company on the Battalion's eastern flank would be attacked; then the command Headquarters, from the rear; and finally the most exposed position, D Company, on the far left. This is the clarity of hindsight. The dynamics of a battlefield have changed little over the centuries, and so, as with

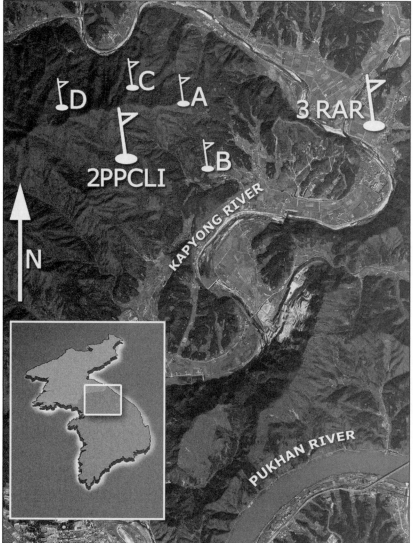

The four 2 PPCLI company positions at Kapyong, with battalion headquarters in the centre, can be seen on this map. Chinese assaults came from the north, first driving the Australians off neighbouring Hill 504, then attacking PPCLI's B Company, then battalion headquarters from the rear, and finally D Company, which called in artillery fire on its own position to prevent being overrun.

most battles anywhere since the Siege of Troy, the action at Kapyong on the night of April 24 was fought amidst great chaos and confusion.

114

Most individual soldiers in any battle know only what's happening a few metres around them. Kapyong was fought in the dark, which only added to the terror.

Bill Chrysler: "We knew our position was on the main route into Seoul. It just had to be held. Stone told us that we simply had to hold. Stone was sitting there in a chair, rocking back and forth with a rifle in this lap, saying, "Let the bastards come! Nobody leaves!"[12]

Charles Petrie, a lieutenant in B Company, on the opposite side of the hill: "As we were moving into position some guys wondered, *what the hell am I doing here*? But once the shooting started you knew damned well what you're doing there; looking after your own tail. It became pretty clear."[13]

Jim Stone explained the gravity of their situation with crisp clarity.

Alex Sim: "Colonel Stone came up on the radio stating: 'We're surrounded. We'll hold this position until we're relieved.' Well, I thought about this for a second. The essence of it was: We're surrounded and we're staying here. I called up a buddy on the radio: 'Did you hear that?' I asked him. 'What did you think?' Stone overheard all this and jumped back on his radio set and snapped: 'Get off the air!' So I thought, well I guess we'll hold the position then."[14]

Stone's icy serenity, says Captain Murray Edwards, was contagious: "Stone was a cool soldier. Very cool. Very calm. That rubs off on everyone else. A man under pressure like he was showed he was a true soldier. His whole aim was to control and direct the battle and keep his commanders and the rest calm and not panicky. He was talking with them direct. If they knew he was calm then they'd think there was no reason why they shouldn't be calm too. It was psychology."[15]

The mortar crews dug in their firing positions. Because the terrain was rocky, the ammunition was stored above ground, and exposed, unprotected from explosions and bullets. As the mortar crews dismantled their machine guns from their vehicles, they spotted shadowy figures darting past them in the night. Perhaps they were terrified South Korean soldiers fleeing to safety, but no one knew, and no one was going to go and ask them who they were. They were only about 50 yards away. The mortar crews were very jumpy.

"Some guys could hear the Chinese coming," remembers Smiley Douglas. "But I never heard a thing. I was too goddamned busy digging holes and getting ready, waiting for them to come. They were just over the hill."[16]

The Chinese could be seen silhouetted in the moonlight as they made for the Australians on the next hill, where the battle there was in its last desperate stages.

Murray Edwards could listen to company battle reports coming in on the radio at Stone's headquarters. "I'm not ten feet away from Stone. I was just sitting there listening. I was wondering: would they break through or not? The Chinese were going to swamp us with numbers. It didn't matter to them how many casualties they took. We could hear them getting closer and closer."[17]

As an already nervous Bill Chrysler waited by his machine gun, an absolutely chilling sound came out of the night and his heart skipped a beat: "We were overlooking a gully. Something woke me up. Someone out there was calling out: 'Bill Chrysler. Tonight you die!' Somehow they got hold of my name."[18]

His mysterious tormentor was wrong, Bill Chrysler did not die that night, but it was close.

Did Murray Edwards ever think it was hopeless? "No. It never entered your mind any more than we thought we'd lose World War Two. Anybody on the outside wouldn't have given us a hope, but no one on the inside ever thought of losing the war; it was just not possible. Same as in at Kapyong. We never thought we'd be beaten."[19]

Don Hibbs wasn't so sure: "I thought we were never going to make it. I thought, *this is where I'm going to die*. There were just too many of them. Most of the guys had a feeling this was going to be their last day on earth. Maybe we weren't going to be here tomorrow. I believed that we had to go down fighting, you know the old gung-ho, but I wasn't gung-ho, I was praying that I could survive. We weren't going down without a fight but if we're gonna go down, we're not gonna go alone."[20]

Then the fight began. Hibbs continues: "You had keep an eye peeled. They were all over the place. They were everywhere. I didn't really see these guys. I'd see people sometimes by the flash of rifle fire, but you don't know whose it is, yours or theirs."

Make a run for it? Not likely, says Hibbs. "The idea was stay in your trench or get shot. Even your own men would pump one into you. They didn't attack in full force. If they had come in full force, they'd have run over us in twenty minutes. But they came piecemeal and we must have killed thousands."

Don Hibbs paused to reflect, then the Kapyong memories flooded out: "A guy with me went to get ammo because we were running low. He took off. Two or three minutes later a Chinese chap came running over. I pulled the trigger and hit him in the side of his neck. He fell in on top of me so I took his weapon and threw it out. I couldn't bring myself to shoot him again so I waited there until he died. My buddy came back in about eight minutes and I said to him: 'great time to leave.'"

Private Don Worsfold of Victoria recalled, with a hint of poetry, later, "The Chinese were advancing at a solid trot, six abreast," "It is as if we are witnessing disciplined Roman Legions advancing, advancing, advancing … the Chinese are intent on destroying us … I'll tell you this is no moral builder."[21]

Mike Czuboka was resigned to simply toughing it out: "Well, we were trapped. All the roads were controlled by the Chinese. So we had nowhere to go. The idea that we'd withdraw didn't cross our minds. Withdrawal was not an option."[22] The soldiers, he says, had faith in Stone. "But nonetheless, the general feeling was that we were in deep shit."

John Bishop was in A Company. The Chinese mysteriously went around his position. He could deep hear the attacks being mounting on his flanks.

"We could hear them slipping around us," he recalls. "It could have been a patrol or it could have been 10,000 of them. We could not ever actually hear them. What we heard was a sort of muffled sound of feet."[23]

They were skirting around A Company, leaving it out of the battle. They were on their way to take out B Company next door. Bishop followed their scurrying sounds off in the darkness.

"What was running through your mind was: *We are not going to move. We'll probably die here.* This sounds like bullshit now, but we just said, 'No, we'll probably die here.' There was no question about it. We would just stand and fight and die if we have to. But we're going to fight and we're going to make it."[24]

There was never any discussion, Bishop says, of trying to break out. "We were simple boys. We thought we'd have a better chance of survival in staying and fighting together. If we broke up into small units, we'd be birdseed."

Alex Sim managed to snatch a bit of sleep, with one eye open, as he waited for his evening to get interesting: "We had to make the best of it under cover of darkness. I lay down behind some rocks. I didn't expect attack 'til next morning at first light. Suddenly, around 5:30 we came under heavy machine-gun fire 150 yards to our rear! Our rear slope was totally exposed. I yelled to take cover wherever you can. I hide behind a cardboard ration box. At least they can't see me. I could hear the bullets pumping into the ground and whizzing by."[25]

Could he see where the bullets were hitting? "I don't remember looking. I wasn't interested in where they were going as long as it wasn't into me."

At about 9:30 that night, B Company took the brunt of the opening Chinese attack, coming under mortar and machine fire. A half hour later the forward platoon, number 6, under Lieutenant Harold Ross, was being swarmed by about 400 Chinese and was engaging in hand-to-hand combat. The men fought on as long as they could. One section was overrun. Private R.G.H Tolver died, in his trench; as did Corporal C.R. Evans. They were later found, their bodies together. On one of their rifles the woman's name, Lydia, was carved on its wooden stock. Evans was still gripping his weapon, its bayonet piercing an enemy soldier. The dead Chinese also clutched his own rifle, its bayonet run through Evans's body.

The other men, the enemy teeming around them, eventually fixed their bayonets and battled their way back to the main company position. They retook their position in the bloody melee. Two more attacks were repelled with the aid of mortars and machine-gun fire, when many Chinese troops were silhouetted in the moonlight as they crossed the Kapyong River. The next morning more than seventy Chinese dead were counted in front the B position. It's not known how many of their dead the Chinese retrieved and took with them.

It was a harrowing, wild action.

The Chinese used bugles, partly to unnerve their enemy, but also to serve as signals to direct their own men.

> We could hear their bugles. We knew they were coming. But they'd be almost on top of you before you could see them. They wore running shoes and you'd never hear them unless they stepped on a stick. When the attack

started they'd start yelling. As soon as we saw them we'd start firing. We'd be looking down at them. They were coming up out of the darkness. In some cases they'd be right on top of us.

Oh Jesus, it was noisy. We were firing. They were firing. Guys were throwing grenades down the hill and they were going off. Everything you saw, you just shot at. Jesus. We'd just keep firing and they'd keep firing.[26]

One man, after his ammunition ran out, threw his bayonet-tipped rifle like a spear at the Chinese.

Murray Edwards remembers recovering the positions they'd lost and they found "one of our boys there who'd been killed. And he had four dead Chinese around him."[27]

Kim Reynolds from Morse, Saskatchewan, says there was no talk of attempting a breakout. It certainly hadn't saved the British Glosters. The Patricias' best bet was to stick together, "just sweat it out. The Chinese could be very quiet in their running shoes until they were on top of you. All you could see was moving shadows in the moonlight. Your trench was supposed to be four feet deep. Mine was three feet."[28]

The defenders all remember the events differently. Some heard warnings and encouragement shouted back and forth between the rifle positions. There were often yells for help or more ammunition and grenades. Others remember no one saying anything at all and hearing only the sound of gunfire all around.

Don Hibbs: "There were shouts of 'watch yourself!' or 'keep down!' or 'I need ammo' as Chinese infantrymen ran right by our positions."[29]

Alex Sim: "We were looking down. I was always dark down there. It's easier to be low, like they were, looking up; then you could then see people outlined on the skyline. But we were looking down."[30]

But the idea was to be on the high ground. Make him come up at you and tire himself out. Make the enemy come at you in the open where he'd have no cover. Make him as terrified as you are.

"We couldn't see them at first," says Sim. "But we could hear them. They blew bugles. They had a philosophy that blowing bugles and making noise fear puts into the enemy. We had knots in the pits of our stomachs."

While some Patricias remember hearing little during the fighting, it was not the same for Alex Sim: "You could hear and talk to guy in same trench. I could quite clearly hear someone shouting: 'The Chinese are coming! The Chinese are coming!'"

Kim Reynolds recalls, however, "being encouraged not to talk so the enemy couldn't hear and locate you."[31]

Lieutenant Charles Petrie was in charge of B Company's 6 Platoon. He discouraged wild firing into the darkness: "Someone would fire a rifle. I would say: 'So, show me the body.' I didn't like people discharging at night because the muzzle flash would tell somebody else where you are."[32]

But if soldiers were in doubt about who and what was out there, and felt they were in danger, with their lives and their buddy's lives at stake, then they would open up. Hitting a "friendly" by mistake was a risk everyone simply accepted and lived with.

"You don't take chances." says Petrie. "If you get suspicious, you shoot first. You've a 50-50 chance at them, so try to make your chances a little better that you'll be the one not done in. If you were not there at Kapyong you tend to assume those that we who were know everything that's going on. But we didn't. If someone gets shot up by friendly fire, well, you can't pay attention to that. You're focused on the other fellows who are trying to do you in."

In the reality of Kapyong, nowhere was safe. Even in C Company, which did not come under direct attack, life was perilous, as Al Lynch learned: "I couldn't dig much of a foxhole. I was on solid rock. I could go down maybe six inches. I was really exposed. I had no cover. I was sitting in the open, really. I could see the soldiers. I could hear the 'pop, pop, pop' as a sniper was firing at me."[33]

In A and C companies, which were not actually under attack, the men there could tell by listening to the steadily rising tempo of the gunfire that the battle over in B's position was reaching a critical stage. Soon the sounds they were hearing were not just mortar and rifle fire. Intermixed increasingly were the dull thumps of hand grenades. Grenades are a close-up weapon. Unlike the movies, in real-life they are not used to blow up tanks and bridges. They are what's called anti-personnel weapons. They are used to blow up people. If the men in

B Company were defending themselves with grenades, it could only mean the Chinese were almost on top of their positions, or perhaps even in among them.

Corporal Bill Shuler, from Chapeau, Quebec, even though he was a medic, was told that every man was needed to defend B Company's position. He was shot at repeatedly as he darted back and forth to attend casualties. In the hand-to-hand fighting that followed, he killed two enemy soldiers.

In the midst of the crisis, young Wayne Mitchell from Vancouver virtually stepped out of a Hollywood movie and right into 2 PPCLI legend.

A member of a light machine gun crew, his foxhole was overrun.

As 100 Chinese attacked his position, the official citation which describes what Mitchell does next is something out of Hemmingway.

> Not withstanding the overwhelming odds, with marked determination he held his ground, skilfully using his Bren [light machine gun] to inflict maximum casualties on the enemy. He was largely responsible for repulsing this attack and was wounded in the chest during the course of the battle. Although wounded, he refused to leave his Bren gun and was a source of inspiration to the remainder of the platoon.
>
> He was ordered to report to Platoon headquarters to have his wounds dressed. He voluntarily carried a wounded comrade back to safety.
>
> By 2400 hours [midnight] the Chinese had overrun two sections of 6 Platoon and were attacking Platoon Headquarters. Private Mitchell again skilfully brought his Bren gun into action to repulse this attack. At one stage seeing his Platoon Sergeant with six wounded men pinned down by enemy fire, voluntarily, without regard for his safety, he rushed toward the enemy firing his Bren gun from the hip thus allowing the wounded to be moved to safety. In this action Mitchell was wounded for a second time by an enemy grenade.[34]

By one o'clock in the morning, Platoon headquarters and one section were still holding out, but their ammunition was almost exhausted. The Platoon commander ordered his men to move to cover that was marginally safer, at least for the moment.

It's hard to grasp that all this wild combat is real life and not from some war novel. And it goes on. Mitchell simply would not stay down.

"During the withdrawal, Private Mitchell exposed himself again and again, moving from fire position to fire position, where he could best engage the enemy to cover the withdrawal," continues his citation, which is the longest of all the citations for bravery that night at Kapyong.

"At 0300 hours, after the fourth attack has been repulsed Mitchell had his wounds dressed by the Company medical assistant, but refused to be evacuated and stayed at his Bren gun post for the remainder of the night.... [At] daylight Private Mitchell could hardly stand for loss of blood."[35]

Mitchell was awarded the Distinguished Conduct Medal, second only to the Victoria Cross. He was nineteen.

"He was doing a cowboy trick," says Kim Reynolds. "He was shooting from the hip. I'll tell you he had guts."[36]

For soldiers wounded when the bullets were flying, chances are they were on their own until the fighting ebbed away. As Alex Sim saw, there was only so much that could be done while the fighting raged: "Every company had stretcher bearer. In a lull, they'd patch people up that were near them. But while the fight was going on, if you were wounded, you sort of just lay there and bleed or tried to patch yourself up. You couldn't expect much help until the battle ended."[37]

Even the terse, clipped language of the battalion's official War Diary, written that same night, conveys the drama that was unfolding:

> At approximately 2100 hours Major C.V. Lilley, MC, CC
> B Coy reported a concentration of 400 Chinese on the
> flat ground below his forward position and asked for
> arty and mortar concentrations on this area., by 2200
> hours the forward platoon commanded by Lt. H. Ross
> was being engaged with increasing ferocity and by 2230
> hrs Major Lilley reported that his forward platoon had
> been partly over-run and was pulling back.[38]

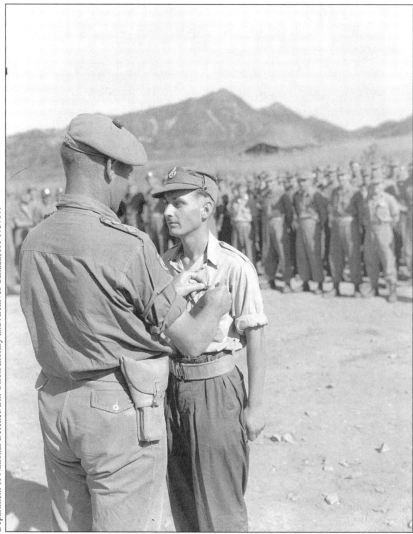

Department of National Defence/Bill Olson/Library and Archives Canada, PA-173707.

Brigadier General John Rockingham gave the Distinguished Conduct Medal to Private Wayne Mitchell for his amazing feats of courage during Kapyong. The diminutive Mitchell was said to have been more nervous during the ceremony than during the battle.

Through the cryptic military abbreviations and jargon, dynamic phrases leap out of the War Diary like newspaper headlines: "… attempt to infiltrate Battalion area … fierce nature of the fighting … casualty figures difficult to obtain … machine guns of the mortar platoon engaged enemy … unknown results … bright moonlight silhouetted the Chinese … overrun … completely overrun … platoon cut off … both members of the MMG were killed at their gun."[39]

Bob Menard, a bazooka expert from Sault Ste. Marie, Ontario, can scarcely remember his night on Kapyong. His recollections are a series of memory flashes: blinding light from explosions and roaring sounds that were meshed into a rolling symphony of noise.

"They were coming at us like ants," he says. "There was so much noise I couldn't make anything out. If anyone was yelling for help, you'd never hear them unless it was your buddy beside you. I was throwing hand grenades by the box."[40]

At one point, a platoon moving in the B Company area stumbled by accident into a zone they had rigged earlier with their own booby-trapped hand grenades strung out inside tin cans. The idea was to provide protection against enemy infiltrators. It was a simple but effective system. When a string was trampled or pulled the grenades would fall free, releasing the detonation lever and arming the grenade to explode in a few seconds.

But a B Company patrol accidently tripped a grenade. One man was killed, another injured in the throat. A quick-thinking sergeant took out a pen, broke off the end, and shoved it into the wound, allowing the wounded man to breathe.

Smiley Douglas, a farm boy from Alberta, had helped lay out the minefield and had seen the trouble coming too late.

What happened next was right out of a movie and cannot be explained by logic or reasoning or even training, for there was too little time for such factors to come into play. What Smiley Douglas did next speaks to his character and his instinct for sacrifice, an unconscious awareness to know what is the simply the right and selfless thing to do.

"Someone yelled at me: 'Douglas, stop them guys!' So that's what I did. I ran up there as hard as I could to catch them. I was too damn late. They'd already tripped one grenade."[41]

Then, a second grenade flipped free from its tin-can restraint.

> I seen it and they didn't. I told them: "Hit the dirt you guys!" I ran in over top of these three guys who were knocked down by the first grenade. I saw the second

one. I yelled at the rest of them to lie down. I grabbed
for it, picked it up, and tried to throw it away. I was
too damn slow.

I didn't have time to think. I did what comes naturally.
It went off right in my hand. It knocked me down, but
didn't knock me out. But I couldn't get up because my leg
was knocked up. I probably said "Goddamn." I don't know,
probably what I said was worse than that. Don Pennell
took his laces out of his boots to make a tourniquet.

I can't remember anything after that. Next thing I
remember is waiting for a helicopter to come and pick
me up. Just like those MASH helicopters you see on TV.

He had lost an arm and seriously injured his legs to save his friends.
He was taken to a field hospital run by doctors in the Indian Army, for
whose care he has the highest praise.

Smiley Douglas was awarded the Military Medal. His commendation reads that he, "by his own brave act and complete disregard for his
own safety undoubtedly saved the lives of the men in question."

It had been a gruelling night for B Company: four killed and ten
wounded. But they had held.

Everyone knew that, being surrounded, there would be no resupply.
They'd have to make do with what they'd brought to the top of the hill.

Charles Petrie: "Most contacts lasted about ten minutes. My longest lasted maybe forty-five minutes. Time gets compressed. Firing was
on again/off again. Let's face it; you've only so much ammunition. Every
man had 200 rounds. You've no idea how quickly you can fire that off."[42]
Contacts are unexpected clashes with the enemy involving small units.
For example, engagements between platoons and patrols would be contacts, but it would not describe battles involving divisions, which have
thousands of men.

The Chinese, with primitive communications and few radios, were
relying on a simple tactic: to overwhelm the Canadians and crush them
by sheer weight of numbers before the Patricias could react. Against a
confused or frightened foe, it might have worked. Against B Company,
it did not.

But for the Patricias, the night was only just beginning.

The Chinese were now preparing to sweep their attack one stage to the west, to manoeuvre down and work around the beleaguered B Company on the far right of the hill, and to get in behind the Battalion's vital command post in the centre, where Stone was directing the defence, and force a way in the lightly-defended back door. Everyone on Kapyong knew the centre simply must hold, or the whole position, and by extension that entire part of the front, would be lost. And the road to Seoul would be open.

Over at A Company, on the northern edge of the position, some of Owen Browne's men could tell that Stone and his headquarters to their south were in danger of being infiltrated, and the men opened fire into the darkness to try to give support.

Stone grabbed his radio and, as Browne sheepishly wrote years later, barked:

> "What's going on over in A Company?" I repeated my recently acquired intelligence of infiltrating enemy who even now were approaching his tactical HQ.
>
> "Well stop your firing you bloody fool. We can take care of ourselves. Save your ammunition. You're going to need it."[43]

As it turned out, A Company was not attacked and they did not need to ration their ammunition, but they did feed much of it over to besieged D Company when they were swarmed. But that was later. Now the crisis was with Stone's headquarters, where Chinese raiders circled around the entire Canadian position to attempt to storm through from the south, the position with the thinnest defences.

At that point, everything depended on about a dozen or so men.

They were the crews of the mortar platoon, dug in about 218 yards from headquarters. Their transportation was "half-tracks," highly mobile trucks with conventional front wheels and caterpillar tracks on the back, ideal for cross-country travel at high speed. They were used to carrying both the mortar crews and their mortars and bombs. Each half track was armed with a .50-calibre machine gun (and a lighter .30-calibre medium machine gun) that fired a bullet the size of a man's thumb. Lieutenant Hub Gray from Calgary was in charge of these lethal heavy-duty killers. It was these guns and their crews that would save battalion headquarters.

"It is an eerie sight," Gray wrote in his first-hand account of the battle. "Five hundred men advancing towards us and not a discernable sound from any of them…. It is as though we are watching unheralded ghosts silently floating up the hill intent on harvesting their prey. The sobering reality is they aren't ghosts, they are very real soldiers carrying automatic weapons and they are hell bent on killing us."[44]

Gray ordered his men to cock their weapons, but hold their fire, as the infiltrators came agonizingly close, unaware they were entering a lethal ambush. The enemy was only about 110 yards away. Then Gray gave the order to open up, "smashing huge swaths through the Chinese ranks."

Bill Chrysler was breathless: "It's unbelievable how close they were to us. When Hub ordered us to open up, I opened up on them and my shots going high at first till I got their range. They knew they were being hit by something that's for sure. We could hear screaming and hollering from their wounded. It lasted a very short time."[45]

Mortar crewman Mike Czuboka says Hub Gray was one of the real heroes of Kapyong: "We were saved by those .50 calibres. About 500 Chinese started climbing towards us. Hub Gray lined them up with six 50-mg's. If it hit you it would blow you apart. Hub waited till they were fairly close. Then they were all just splattered all over the place."[46]

Chrysler compared it to hitting ducks in a shooting gallery. "It was a great thing to see them tumbling down. We were running out of ammo and couldn't have kept it up much longer. I had about a half a box left. If we'd run out of ammo we had orders to fix bayonets."[47]

Private Jim Wall from Winnipeg said it looked like "a bunch of ants groping their way up the hill. It is frightening watching them slowly ascend, and to realize they are coming to kill us. When Gray orders the machineguns to fire it is as though someone had kicked the top off an anthill. There are masses of fallen, dead and wounded. Those left standing, grab what they can of their casualties and are running and tumbling down the hill as fast as their legs can carry them, towards the river. I am one happy soldier."[48]

The machine-gun and mortar fire saved battalion headquarters. Perhaps as many as four hundred enemy soldiers had been stopped cold by a handful of Patricias. The .50-cals literally blew the Chinese back down the ravine. The mortar explosions and tracer bullets lit up the darkness of the ravine much like a flickering strobe light. It was a terrifying sight.

The machine guns defending the headquarters was one of a several crucial moments in the battle that were pivotal; where everything could have turned out differently, and turned out worse.

> In my opinion the .50 calibre and .30 calibre machine guns firing in unison near the tactical HQ saved all of us at Kapyong," says Mike Czuboka "Their vicious firepower is thunderous and overwhelming. It is fascinating watching the various fire patterns, the trajectory of the machine gun tracers is so close they are almost firing upon us. The Chinese having already suffered heavy losses must have felt they had suddenly encountered a power and well-armed enemy. I felt very relieved when it was over for they were advancing uphill in the rear of our position … it was a very close thing.[49]

Then, the mortar crews, until then supporting B Company to their right, turned their weapons completely around and fired almost straight up so the explosives would come down almost in front of them, shattering the Chinese now almost on top of their own position. Their mortar barrels were burning hot.

Mike Czuboka's men worked at breakneck speed, hoping to avoid a double feed in which a second mortar is dropped down the barrel before the one before it has been fired off. A double feed would not only kill the crew, but would detonate the remaining mortar bombs stored out on the open ground nearby. Such a blast would wipe out the whole platoon and the headquarters would be at the mercy of the Chinese coming in the back door.

Mike Czuboka had the blind optimism of youth: "I was nineteen. The world looks a lot different when you're nineteen. You don't die when you're nineteen. It's other people who die."[50]

This was the vantage point of D Company, on the west side of Kapyong, where the Chinese made their most intense attack.

The attack resulted a great loss to the Chinese and none to the Canadians. Some Chinese, Chrysler remembers, surrendered out of nowhere, only twenty or so feet away.

Czuboka is convinced the Chinese attackers had no idea how vulnerable the Patricias had been and assumed they had huge resources, which they definitely did not. But the attack had been beaten back and the Chinese would not try that route again. The attack on the mortar platoon was all over in about ten brutal minutes. It had all been, as Wellington said after Waterloo, a very close-run thing. And there was more to come. This would be the most harrowing yet.

On the far west of the hill, the most precarious and exposed of the Canadian positions perched on Kapyong, it was now D Company's turn.

The Chinese came at them from three sides.

A few minutes earlier, it all depended on protecting B Company. Then it was the headquarters that was crucial. And now everyone, said Mike Czuboka, knew that everything depended on D Company: "If D had been overrun, we were all finished."

It seemed that whatever was under attack at any given moment was the key to everything.

At D Company, their plight couldn't have been more perilous.

One Patricia, although he continued to fight, remembers nothing of the battle after the point when he was suddenly covered with pulp when the man next to him took a bullet in the head.

Lance Corporal Bill White's father had been in the Second World War. The military tradition was in his family's blood. Now it was his turn.

> We knew we were in big trouble. We thought we were going to learn how to use chopsticks. I could hear our people hollering as the Chinese were infiltrating us: "They're here! They're here." You could see them. You'd shoot one and the next guy along would pick his rifle up. He'd come and you'd shoot him too. And there'd be another one. Colonel Stone told us we were to take eight of the enemy with us.[51]

No one was keeping exact track, but the Patricias easily met their quota. Two men from D died in their foxhole manning their Vickers machine guns, apparently firing to the end, with an unexpended belt of ammunition still in their weapon. The enemy poured into the area. By three o'clock in the morning, one platoon was cut off and another was being overrun. There was pandemonium in the darkness. The Chinese who killed the two Vickers machine gunners, Maurice Carr and Bruce MacDonald, were themselves killed in a firefight with a crew manning a lighter Bren machine gun. Then one of the Bren crew, Private J.M. Lessard, was killed moments later, hit in the face by a blast from a burp gun. The Chinese were coming in waves. Over the noise of the gunfire, the Patricias could hear the Chinese commanders shouting encouragement to their men, accompanied by trumpets and noisemakers. Insults were hurled back and forth over the din of the battle between Chinese officers and platoon commander Mike Levy, who spoke a Chinese dialect.

The commander of desperate D Company, Captain Wally Mills, had set up his headquarters out of sight of much of his platoon. He could not see his own men and could not personally assess the flow of battle, which was changing by the second. Mills radioed Stone asking for permission to withdraw. Stone curtly turned him down. If D Company's position was lost, the Chinese would occupy high ground looking down on Stone's headquarters and could cut it off from the other companies. The Patricias then would have been methodically slaughtered, as were the Glosters the day before. The headquarters must be held, and D Company was the key to its protection.

At the centre of the crisis was 10 Platoon. Mike Levy was as cool and professional as any soldier in any army in Korea. This was the superb warrior that at sixteen, only six years earlier, had been fighting as a guerrilla against the Japanese.

Levy radioed in for artillery fire to come down on his own Platoon. This was entirely Levy's initiative. Technically the request came from Mills, but in effect he simply passed Levy's request on.

It was a desperate moment. It was a gamble; the barrage may have killed some or all of the defenders. But there would be no doubt at all what would happen if the artillery barrage hadn't been called in. Unless something drastic was done, 10 Platoon would have vanished in the human-wave assaults.

"It's the very last thing you can possibly do," says Murray Edwards.

Then the artillery arrived. Over the next forty minutes, around 4,000 rounds were fired off by 16th Royal New Zealand Artillery Regiment, based just to the south. The barrage rained down on Levy's in his position, who was on his radio constantly, giving directions so the New Zealand artillerymen could adjust their fire. The shells crashed only five or six metres from his men as they hunkered down in their shallow little foxholes scraped out of the rock.

A 10 Platoon rifleman vividly recalled hugging the bottom of his foxhole during the shelling: "Our slit trenches were within hollering distance, when we got the word, we all crouched down in the trench. The artillery dropped a ten minute barrage on top of us. It stopped that attack, but the Chinese came at us again. They were about to overrun us, when another ten minute barrage came in. Later, we were hard pressed and called in a third ten minute barrage. We were convinced the artillery would kill us all, but there were no direct hits on any of the slit trenches. The Chinese, caught out in the open, were stopped cold."[52]

Levy kept his unit together, fighting constantly through it all. It was classic leadership that is a product of character rather than training.

Mike Levy did not need rank to have authority. He reeked of "presence." Rock stars don't have charisma; Mike Levy had charisma. Such dynamic leaders simply sweep their followers along with them as they surge forward. One admirer was Charles Petrie.

"Levy was a real crackerjack. He spoke Cantonese. In previous fights among the hills a week earlier, his platoon would get annoyed that he was shouting insults at the enemy in Chinese. The Chinese would respond. He'd stirred up a hornets' next. He was a natural leader. He knew which way was up."[53]

Years later, in 1997, Levy provided a private account to a friend of the attack on his lonely position. It's a terse, to-the-point description of a harrowing night with 10 Platoon. Levy would have made a terrific journalist. His story crackles with tension and menace and takes the reader along on every dash for cover and each machine-gun burst. Because this platoon's story is so dramatic a part of the entire Kapyong story, Levy's description is a riveting glimpse of battle from the inside, looking out.

Levy had no idea where his company commander, Captain Mills, was located. At about 1:30 a.m., one of Levy's corporals reported hearing noises to their front and just down below. Levy called in artillery and mortar fire, and his submachine gun crew opened up. He then moved up to be with his most forward riflemen.

"By this time," he says, "all kinds of firing is directed at us, mainly coming from in front 30 or 40 yards away."[54]

The artillery fire was coming in too far forward. He radioed that it should be adjusted closer in.

"The enemy was charging en masse, 30 to 50 men at a time, charging at us in waves.… we rolled grenades down on them. As the battle became more intense I kept calling for more artillery and mortar fire, adjusting the fire, gradually creeping closer and closer to my platoon."

Levy was in the thick of it, darting, out in the open, going from foxhole to foxhole to direct fire where it was most needed. Despite the artillery and mortar bombardment, the enemy was closing in. Fire from one of Levy's machine gun crews sliced into the Chinese flank. For a moment, there was a short lull as the Chinese attempted to recover from their confusion.

"Agonizing screaming came from their wounded and the shouting of orders from the enemy lines," he says. "A Chinese officer was demanding his troops advance with greater aggression on our position to 'Kill the American pigs.' Being conversant in Chinese, I shouted back: 'We are Canadian soldiers … we have lots of Canadian soldiers here.'"

The enemy commander then told his men not to listen to "that 'Son of a Turtle,' a tremendous insult in Chinese. Attack. Attack. Kill them.'"

Levy and Chinese officer flung insults back and forth at each other until one of Levy's men told him to cut it out because it was simply infuriating the enemy even more.

By three o'clock in the morning, the intensity of the attacks was white hot and 12 Platoon on Levy's right was overrun.

"Soon after their machine gun ceased firing we heard a voice down below and to our right shouting 'Don't shoot. We're coming up.' Four men from 12 Platoon including Private Barwise and two Koreans came into our position. They reported two machine gunners had been killed and overrun."

Levy's immediate superior, Captain Wally Mills, told him to be prepared to move back. But Levy didn't know where Mills was located, nor where the other two platoons were dug in. Mills had never held discussions with his platoon commanders about such a contingency. Levy had no idea what was happening beyond a few feet on either side of him, outside his own violent little universe. Was the company's position falling? Or was the entire battalion collapsing? Was he to be the last to leave? If they were to withdraw, then to where?

Meanwhile, the enemy pressed on with their attacks. Stone rejected Mill's request to pull out. "Nobody could pull out. If we lose that hill, we lose it all," said Stone.[55]

Stone's instincts, as usual, were bang on.

Levy twice more called for more artillery and mortar fire.

> I spoke to the men, encouraging them and telling them
> supporting fire was coming in, to get down. I moved
> the artillery five up or down, left or right, depend-
> ing on where I could see them massing, and again
> on charging our position … I kept calling for more

close-in supporting fire. During the course of the battle throughout the night I called for supporting fire 30
to 40 times … we were now cut off from the remainder
of the Company.[56]

Because the Chinese were virtually on top of them, when the artillery rounds came roaring in some men didn't hug the ground when Levy
ordered them to do so. Many of the rounds had "variable time fuses"
and burst a few feet above the ground and were much more lethal than
ground burst shells which explode on impact with the soil.

The concussion grabs Clouthier and Baxter as though
by the scruff of their necks, tossing them up in the air
and slamming them down hard. Clouthier falls under
Baxter, the Bren (light machine gun) crashing down
on top of them. Baxter is up immediately shouting
for Simpson who's at the bottom of the trench, to load
more magazines as he fires off continuing bursts … the
Chinese, running through the barrage ignoring fallen
comrades, are but seven metres to the front.[57]

At 11 Platoon, a direct mortar hit killed the two-man machine gun
crew. The position was manned by a new crew, who had to drag the bodies of the slain men out of the foxhole. Because of the sleep sloop, their
bodies tended to roll down the hillside until they were finally anchored
at the base of some shrubs.

Back at 10 Platoon, Levy and another soldier were running an ammo
shuttle service between the men in the foxholes and about ten men he
was keeping in reserve a few yards behind. The men in reserve were
feverishly reloading machine-gun magazines, which were then handed
out by Levy where the need was greatest. He was also replacing wounded
men with those in reserve. Then the reserve section ran out of ammunition. Then yet another Chinese charge came at them, this time from
three directions. There was a crisis at hand as events unravelled very rap-
idly. It's hard to grasp now that this chilling real-life thriller was being
played out in a Forgotten War.

Levy's heart-pounding account continued: "I have no idea of their numbers for I am too busy defending our position. Our firing slowed them down, but did not stop their advance. I called once more the artillery and mortar fire to impact as close as I dared, about 15 yards to our front ... I moved from sector to sector trying to concentrate the artillery to be most effective."[58]

This is where the bolt-action Lee-Enfield rifles of the Patricias were utterly the wrong kind of weapon for this kind of fight.

> We ran out of grenades. Their numbers were such that our small arms (Lee-Enfields) and light machine guns was insufficient to stop them. We were being hit by small arms, Burp guns, light machine guns, medium machine guns and mortar fire. It was a very close call. It was imperative the artillery and mortar support rain down with the greatest intensity and as close as possible. I moved constantly from point to point in an endeavour to concentrate the artillery where it was crucial to do so.

It worked. By six o'clock in the morning, the Chinese gave up trying. It had simply been too much. The New Zealand artillery gunners and the Patricias' own mortar crews on the other side of the hill had broken the back of the assault. It had been terrifying for Levy and his men, but worse for the enemy. Caught in the open, they were decimated. Some Canadians were slightly injured by their own artillery, but none were killed. The position would hold, for now.

The Patricias were still surrounded, and it was still a dangerous neighbourhood. Chinese snipers remained on the job. Levy's men were out of grenades and almost out of ammunition. Soldiers from other Companies brought over ammo cases and some men were still being wounded as they lugged it through the gullies and over the rocks.

At the centre of the story of D Company lies one of the mysteries of Kapyong.

Captain Wally Mills, commanding officer of D Company, was awarded the Military Cross, getting credit for calling in the artillery on his own positions, even though he'd done little more than pass information between his platoons and support units. Mike Levy, in fact, was the actual man-on-the-spot in the centre of the fighting, and it was he who had actually requested his own positions be shelled. And it was Levy and his men, not Mills, who would be coming under shellfire. Yet Levy received no recognition for his heroism, nor did he personally seek any. The indifference of the brass to Levy's remarkable role was then, and remains today, inexplicable.

The Canadian Army's official history of the Korean War, *Strange Battleground*, weirdly deals with the whole amazing episode about D Company's shelling in a single, terse, soulless paragraph:

> At this critical moment Captain Mills requested the artillery to lay down defensive fire on top of his position and after two hours succeeded in stemming the enemy's advance. Undeterred by these reverses, the enemy persisted in his attacks, but was driven off each time by artillery fire. At last, with the approach of daylight, the pressure subsided, and "D" Company was able to re-establish itself in its previous position. Captain Mills was awarded the Military Cross for his bravery in this action.[59]

There is not a whisper of Mike Levy in Canada's official story of the war.

Ironically, Levy's heroism is recognized in the Australian official history of the Korean War, which notes he issued a unique order for an artillery barrage on his own foxholes that lasted forty minutes.

Many on Kapyong that night were (and are) puzzled by events that led to the artillery barrage on D Company.

"Mills not that amenable to advice," says one surviving officer today. "Mills was happy he didn't have to stick his nose above the parapet while Mike conducted the battle. We were having trouble figuring out what the devil was going on in D Company. Something was funny. Something was suspicious. We were a bit surprised when Wally got his MC. There was a sense something wasn't quite so smooth over there in D."[60]

Definitely there was something strange happening, or not happening, on Kapyong's western flank.

There were many, even at the time of the battle, who were alarmed at what they could make out of events over on that isolated left flank, where D Company was fighting it out on its own. Major Gordon Henderson, the battalion's battle adjutant, was in continual radio communication with Mills, D Company's commander.

"I passed the information to Lieut Colonel Stone, who was commanding the battle," Henderson wrote in a letter years later. "I could not understand why, when I asked (Mills) for a situation report, there were long pauses. Frequently answers were vague. Reports from other Companies were precise and quickly given. Now I understand ... Mills could not see any of the battle taking place at his platoons. Captain Mills had to check with Lieut Mike Levy and other platoon commanders to be updated. They in turn were busy controlling their fight with the Chinese."[61]

Ominously, Henderson continues, at Stone's headquarters no one could figure out exactly what was going on with D Company and which decisions were being made by the captain nominally in command, or by the platoon lieutenants, such as Levy who called in artillery and mortar fire on his own men.

After the fighting ended, Henderson and Stone sat down and analyzed the battle.

"There was a lot of talk about D Company," Henderson writes. "When we were finished Stone got up and said 'As far as Mills is concerned I don't know whether to court martial him or put him in for a decoration.'"[62]

Mills got his decoration.

Mike Levy himself, who rarely talked about Kapyong with anyone, confided to a friend many years later that "Mills never came to our position nor did he at any time call an O Group [an operations meeting where junior officers are given their orders] nor inquired how we had positioned ourselves. I do not believe Mills knew exactly where we dug in."[63]

Levy said no one ever consulted him or asked him to write a report about his actions on Kapyong. No senior officer ever asked him for an account about what had happened. Nor did Wally Mills, the captain who got the decoration, ever speak to Levy about it. Only one officer, a Major Bob Swinton, who had missed the battle, asked Levy about his platoon's actions on that night. Swinton, said Levy "then approached Col Stone, who advised Swinton he would not discuss the matter further."[64]

For decades, no one paid any attention to Mike Levy's bravery. He never spoke of it and he was never asked. He was the forgotten hero of Kapyong, an injustice not made right until over a half century later when Hub Gray, who fought at Kapyong, campaigned passionately to throw light on Levy's pivotal role. Gray tracked down and interviewed some seventy survivors of the battle and wrote a stirring account, *Beyond the Danger Close*, drawing attention to Levy's neglected valour. Finally, in 2003, thanks largely to Gray's efforts, the governor general at the time, Adrienne Clarkson, granted Levy a coat of arms for his valour at Kapyong, with the motto "I Have Prevailed." Clarkson, who was twelve years old at the time of the battle, is today the PPCLI's colonel-in-chief. So modest and unassuming a man was Levy that he wanted to spare the governor general making the presentation trip to British Columbia herself, so instead his new coat of arms was actually delivered by the chief herald of Canada, Robert Douglas Watt. The design includes a lightning flash representing the wireless radio Levy used to call in artillery fire, and Korean pine cones, the official tree of the county of Kapyong.

———

Throughout the night of the 24th and on into the 25th there was more skirmishing and rifle fire, but the assault on D Company would now subside, although no one on the hill could know it at the time.

The artillery salvos on top of 10 Platoon had been another scarcely believable Kapyong moment from a war movie. And there was yet another one on its way.

The exhausted defenders of 10 Platoon were almost out of ammunition. Levy noticed some bandoliers lying in an abandoned foxhole, and asked for volunteers to bring them in.

Ken Barwise stepped forward and straight into history. Barwise had a pathetic childhood. Raised as an orphan, he later did a stint in a reform school, and never received proper schooling. He was a troubled youngster. As a teenager he served on merchant steamers, sailing the globe, then worked in sawmills. Rootless and restless, the Korean War broke out and changed his life. He enlisted in the special force. The army became his home, and he stayed there for thirty years. He was a popular and likeable soldier. That night on Kapyong also made him a memorable one.

Barwise, a towering mountain of man known as the "friendly giant," was an easy target on the battlefield. He ran the gauntlet of enemy fire to grab armfuls of bandoliers and returned yet again to bring back batches of hand grenades. Enemy soldiers blazed away at him the whole time.

Murray Edwards described Barwise chasing the Chinese away by throwing hand grenades at them. "Now that was bravery," says Edwards. "It was also just plain mad."[65]

Barwise became another decorated hero that night, receiving the Military Medal. In addition to retrieving the ammunition, his citation also credits him with killing six Chinese, spraying them at close range as he recovered a captured machine gun and lugged it back to his position.

The commendation declares that his complete disregard for his personal safety under fire: "was an inspiration to his comrades and contributed largely to the successful and the gallant stand made by the Battalion at Kapyong." The man who recommended Barwise for his medal was Mike Levy. (Some would later argue Barwise should have received the Victoria Cross.)

———

The exhausted defenders had survived this long, but they were cut off and running out of almost everything except stamina. It was impossible to determine how much damage they'd been inflicting on the Chinese, who normally retrieved their dead. But in front of Mike Czuboka's mortar and machine gun position, for example, "there were lots of bodies lying around. One guy went out and counted. After a hundred he just quit."[66]

But they essentially were still in the same conundrum as when they started, except now with less of everything to fight with. John Bishop didn't like the looks of their chances of making it through another attack.

"We were just about out of ammo," he says. "If they'd continued, it would have been all over for us. Things got very quiet. We were waiting for the next big push. We felt the bastards were going to come at us with more than ever. We stayed in our trenches. Chinese were still around. If you wandered off, you'd never come back."[67]

Don Hibbs thought time was on the Chinese side, especially if they weren't concerned with casualties: "We couldn't get out. If they'd have had another thousand men, they'd have wiped us out."[68]

Bill Chrysler wondered if he was seeing his last sunrise. "Did I ever think this is it? Well, many things went through my mind. I was twenty. I wondered if I would make it to twenty-one."[69]

As daylight began, they were a ragtag sight. Don Hibbs remembered his Kapyong morning as one to forget: "We were dirty and stinky. Your mouth was dry. We'd had no time to eat, unless it was a biscuit. We had some of our field rations left, but food wasn't on our minds."[70]

Al Lynch, with great foresight, had brought along his Hershey bars into battle. "We didn't have any real food for a couple of days, but I had my chocolate bars."[71]

And now the Patricias steeled themselves for another assault. They hadn't come through all this to give up their hill now. They were up for the fight to come, ignoring the bodies of the Chinese they'd killed, lying among them. In addition, they had on their hands their own soldiers with gunshot wounds; their supplies of food, water, and ammo were all but gone; and they were still in the same position they'd started out in yesterday: surrounded, cut off, and alone. And it seemed yesterday was another universe, light years away.

There was a spooky feel to it all. Some remember Kapyong as a tidy battlefield as battlefields go. They have no memory of the forward slopes of the hill being littered with discarded ammunition crates, bandages, brass ammo casings, and other debris of the fighting. They'd been ordered to keep such junk out of sight so their positions would be harder to detect. Others recall the opposite, especially around the platoons of D and B Company where the fighting had been fiercest. Some Patricias remember seeing no Chinese dead although there had been a great many killed. But others saw mountains of corpses. The fronts of D Company's foxholes were littered with dead. One section of ten men had 200 bodies piled up around it. It was impossible to tell who'd been mowed down by Patricia rifle fire and who died in the New Zealand artillery blasts. To one soldier "it looked like a badly run graveyard."

Charles Petrie over at B Company recalls that his men buried twenty-two Chinese soldiers who were lying among their trenches, simply to get rid of the decaying bodies.

Although the Patricias were strangely upbeat, their situation was still grave. At least yesterday they were fresh and well-armed; now they were not.

Bill White had virtually no ammo left: "I was down to five or six rounds and I [had] no grenades left. We had only our pigstickers, our bayonets. But we weren't going to give up that easily."[72]

Alex Sim's men, despite the intensity of their own firefights on the east of the position, were among those taking their remaining ammunition and grenades over D Company on the west, where they were down to their rounds.

"We shook hands and said farewell," he says. "If another attack came in on D, we probably wouldn't meet again the next morning."[73]

What no one knows is what they were thinking over there on what is termed "the other side of the hill," but Stone had to assume the worst. Additional attacks would be almost impossible to hold off for long because the Chinese could simply keep on throwing up a limitless supply of men at the lonely Canadians on the hill. There was a mathematical neatness to predicting just how such an equation would end, but Stone had faith in his soldiers and they had faith in each other. They could hold out, he was certain, but they couldn't fight for long on what they had left.

At about four o'clock in the morning of the 25th, Stone radioed for resupply: ammunition, food, water, basic medical supplies. Getting to them overland was hopeless because the Chinese controlled the countryside and the primitive roads encircling the Patricias' hill. There was only way possible to get these to surrounded troops: an airdrop. And it had to be done very quickly, before the Chinese realized that one more major, brutal, desperate push could do the trick.

In a remarkable feat of organization, communication, and logistics, the U.S. Air Force put together their rescue package, loaded the aircraft up, and then flew them straight from Tokyo to the skies over Kapyong. Only six hours after Stone first radioed his SOS, planes were swooping in over the hills.

For the men on the hilltop it spelled life. It meant they would not die; at least not die today.

Today, they disagree on how many planes came to save them. Some saw one. Others saw three. In fact there were four. And they were beautiful, they said, and flown by angels.

Of all the terrifying events on Kapyong over the past hours, those

American planes winging in towards their hilltop are the images the Canadian soldiers retain in their minds with the greatest clarity and joy.

The aircraft came in low and slow, and at great risk to being hit by antiaircraft fire.

They appeared first as tiny silver fish in the sky.

Alex Sim: "I was just sitting on side of hill, just looking around. Then these C-119s flew over and all of a sudden these parachutes blossomed out in the sky. I thought: 'We're saved! We're saved.'"[74]

John Bishop: "It was moment of exhilaration. It meant we were still alone but we're not forgotten."[75]

Don Hibbs: "This is good. We're still here and we're still alive."[76]

In Hollywood, there would have been cheering. But when the real thing happened, as Bill Chrysler remembers, no one at Kapyong was cheering. The soldiers just sat quietly, cradling their rifles, and stared, grizzled and red-eyed, up at their salvation: "When we saw those planes we knew we would be okay. We were being re-armed. And the Chinese knew it too. They knew they were up against people who were simply not going to give up."[77]

Rollie Lapointe remembers total quiet on the hill at that moment, except for the aircraft engines. The besieged soldiers, craning their necks, were riveted on the little dots that grew and grew: "Now that was dramatic! They came in low. By Jesus, they were like great big gulls. They dropped their stuff right on our position. I could barely hear them coming in. They just droned a little. It looked like they were not moving at all: Slow, slow, slow. Then they dropped their ass ends and the chutes came out. The Chinese figured the Canadians were here to stay."[78]

Did he jump up and down with glee? No. He was exhausted. "I just sat in my trench and watched."

Canadian artist Ted Zuber painted a dramatic scene of the Kapyong airdrop. It is a popular display at the Canadian War Museum in Ottawa and has become one of the most well-known of all works of Canadian war art. Zuber had been a parachutist and a sniper in Korea, where he was wounded by a grenade. He knows first-hand the sharp thump of explosions and the crack of rifle fire. His Kapyong painting, a dramatic substitute for the combat cameraman who was away on leave, captures the utter isolation of the Patricias on their hilltop, the desolation of their surroundings, and the promise of deliverance those aircraft brought with them.

The Kapyong Patricias owed their lives to those flyers. The pilots' vital re-supply loads dropped, their harrowing mission now completed, they flew off to the horizon and vanished as quickly as they had arrived, forever strangers to the men below. The flyers and their Patricias on the hill, sadly, never met.

An unnatural mood of calm now settled over Kapyong. The Chinese were still out there, harassing the Patricias to keep nerves on edge. Light patrols tried to penetrate D Company but could not penetrate the defensive perimeter. Poor, battered D Company was taking it right to the end. But no further assaults came.

No one knows what the Chinese were making of it all. Was it a good day's work for them? Or was it a debacle? No one knows. They've never released any official account of their version of struggle for Kapyong. They've kept secret their casualty figures, presumably because they were so horrific. Repeated requests to the Chinese government and military for China's version of the Kapyong battle, or for any comment or analysis at all, went unanswered. In light of the estimated 1 million Chinese casualties in the Korean War, Kapyong, with its 5,000 casualties, was a minor affair.

The battle seemed to wind up by increments, and not with a climactic moment. It was a T.S. Eliot ending — not with a bang but with a whimper.

By this time, on the 25th, two tough American Army Rangers had made their way through to the beleaguered Patricias. They were the advance team to provide radio contact with an American Regimental Combat Team scheduled to relieve the Patricias the following day. Both men, a sergeant and a staff sergeant, were seasoned, battle-wise Second World War veterans. Lieutenant Charles Petrie of B Company put them up in a foxhole next to his own and loaned them some Canadian hand grenades, much prized by U.S. infantrymen. There were still minor firefights in the night in which you could still get killed, but compared to what they'd just been through, it was scarcely noticed. Petrie jotted down his recollections of this last night on Kapyong with his American guests:

The night of the twenty-fifth again was very dark with broken cloud and marked by quite a bit of movement; frequent shots being fired, followed by me shouting to the rifleman to "Show me the body!" I was worried that muzzle flash would reveal our new positions, and had ordered that grenades be used against intruders. I found that several of the men had been using American hand grenades, and that they were quite often not exploding. I banned the use of these in the platoon. We were not bounced off the position by the probes during the night, and were now facing the new dawn of 26 April.

Before long, we saw a line of [Chinese] troops advancing north along the valley floor, and an American Forward Observer came to our platoon position to direct artillery fire ... We were joined, shortly, by the Commanding Officer of 5 Regimental Combat Team ... Later in the afternoon, before he left, he asked whether we would accommodate a couple of his senior NCOs to provide a radio link over the night, if he placed them under my command ... I was delighted to have another occupied slit trench, and supplied them with #36 grenades. The two American NCOs were delighted to get #36's, which they had met before; because they felt that they were more effective. We had a quiet night.

The cloud cover started to deliver a fine drizzle just after dawn as the two Americans left to rejoin their headquarters,... I was assigned to command the covering force for the battalion withdrawal on what was now 27 April ... We dug in and spent one warm wet night on a wet shale hill, movement about us often heard ...[79]

Some MASH helicopters now risked the trip in and took out the wounded and the dead. By two o'clock in the afternoon, a road to the south had been cleared of the enemy and reopened. Additional supplies were brought up. The worst of the fighting, though not of the war by a long shot, was largely over at Kapyong.

PPCLI Museum and Archives.

This is a rare photo of the Kapyong hillside after the battle. Note the debris and ammunition cases strewn about in front of foxholes. It gives good idea of the steep uphill climb the Chinese had to tackle.

Tension and anxiety began to ooze out of men on the edge of exhaustion. There were a few signs of what would now be termed post traumatic stress disorder, although none were evident during the fighting itself. A few men could remember nothing of the combat at all, although they'd been in the centre of it. Others, in their mind's eye, could later see only snippets of the fighting — sort of a quick out-of-sequence series of snapshots. While some, despite the hours of gunfire and artillery and bayonet fighting, recalled only the magnificent airdrop, their images of the actual fighting sank into a memory black hole. One man simply sat down and dug into his new para-dropped field rations, downing serving after serving and still wanting more.

Bazooka man Bob Menard was assigned to help bring down the Canadian dead from the Kapyong summit to ambulance Jeeps waiting below. The rifles and ammunition of the dead men were kept to be used later if need be (as then seemed likely) by the survivors.

"We were told to clean up the place," recalls Menard. "We brought down the ten bodies, put them in body bags and stacked them in those Jeeps, one on top of the other like cordwood. It was dangerous work. The Chinese were still lurking in the ravines and they were shooting at us while we were bringing down our dead. My buddy right beside me got wounded. Imagine, they shot at us anyway, even while we were getting our friends' bodies."[80]

On April 26, the Patricias had turned their position over to the relieving American unit, and went into reserve. It was over. Almost.

———

What of the still inexplicable mystery surrounding the heroic Lieutenant Mike Levy, and what was going on in 10 Platoon? A disturbing possible key to understanding Levy's shabby treatment can be found in a letter written almost sixty years after the event. Mel Canfield was a private in the Intelligence Section of 2 PPCLI during Kapyong. Among his duties were making entries into the radio logs and keeping track of communications between Stone's command centre and his infantry companies who were in the centre of the fighting, only a few hundred yards away. The official War Diaries compiled later were based on Canfield's entries. Canfield was a fly on the wall — in his words "in close proximity" to Stone.

In 2002, Canfield wrote to Hub Gray, who was researching the Levy story for his book:

> The day after the battle at Kapyong, LCol Stone made a statement which I overheard that has struck in my craw ever since. I do respect Stone for all that he did in Korea and I recognize that all of us, at times, have experienced personal failings. Stone after the battle must have been considering a number of pressing decisions … He did award Capt Wally Mills the MC for the stand of D Company. I do think it possible he may have considering awarding others; however within my hearing he stated:
> "I will not award a medal to a Jew."
> When Stone made the pronouncement, the resonance in his voice violated all the values that I was raised with and left me feeling like a cracked bell. I was upset and it has always remained with me.[81]

Canfield said Stone's remark was "overwhelming intolerant (and) forever incomprehensible to me. Levy's actions may well have been the strongest element in saving our battalion from being engaged in a much larger battle, if not inglorious defeat."

TO   HUB GRAY
       1102 Levis Avenue SW
       Calgary, AB, T2T 1V1   02 04 19

FROM   9010 Ashwell Road
       Chilliwack, BC, V2P 6W4

Dear Hub,

Re: Comments by;
Lieutenant-Colonel James Riley Stone, DSO 2 bars, MC
Commanding Officer
Second Battalion Princess Patricia's Canadian Light Infantry
at the Battle of Kapyong, Korea,
April 23 – 25, 1951

I was then a private solider in the Intelligence Section, 2nd Patricias. I alternated with others during the battle making authorized entries in the Radio Logs; communications between each of the battalion's companies and Tactical Headquarters, located in the signals van; LCol Stone's command centre. In this capacity I was in close proximity with LCol Stone and the Battle Adjutant, Major Gordon Henderson. I was also engaged in entering the Radio Logs in the months preceding Kapyong.

The War Diary entries describing the events of the day during our time in Korea, were, in part, based upon the record of the Radio Logs.

Earlier in Korea, Captain Gordon Turnbull reported to Tactical Headquarters that Lieut Mike Levy, commanding 10 platoon, under performed during the action on Hill 532. Turnbull was Acting Commanding Officer of Dog Company. A Canadian Press article, by war correspondent Bill Boss, written at the time quotes a statement by the Company Sergeant Major, Swede Larson, " The platoons went in with the bayonet. There were torrents of grenades, the Chinese favourite weapon." At this time the majority of grenades utilized by the Chinese were Stun Grenades. The casualties at Hill 532, were disappointingly high; 9 killed and 25 wounded, about one third of the strength of D Company; Stone was visably upset. He immediately removed Turnbull from a combat role to being the administrative officer of the battalion; adjutant. Thereafter, from time to time, in my presence, Stone made reference to "officers under performing." I had the impression Stone was at times frustrated, and that some of this was directed at Levy. Gray, in his book pertaining to the Patricias battle at Kapyong, examines the action at Hill 532, in detail.

This letter from Mel Canfield to Hub Gray describes how he overheard Colonel Jim Stone say he would not recommend Lieutenant Mike Levy for a medal at Kapyong.

The day after the battle at Kapyong LCol Stone made a statement, which I overheard, that has stuck in my craw ever since. I do respect Stone for all that he did in Korea and I recognize that all of us, at times, have experienced personal failings. Stone, after the battle must have been considering a number of pressing decisions he had to make, prior to returning home. Stone left the battalion soon after Kapyong returning to Canada on compassionate grounds because of an urgent family illness concerning one of his children. He did award Capt Wally Mills the MC, for the stand of D Company. I do think it is possible he may have considered awarding others; however, within my hearing he stated:

"I will not award a medal to a Jew."
When Stone made this pronouncement the resonance in his voice
Violated all the values that I was raised with,
And left me feeling like a cracked bell!
I was upset, it has always remained with me."

Here was the commander I respected and admired, with whom I was unified and inspired in fighting to defeat an unforgiving enemy; making an overwhelmingly intolerant remark! If his exclusion was directed at Levy, his observation was, and is forever incomprehensible to me. Levy actions may well have been the strongest element in saving our battalion from being engaged in a much larger battle, if not an inglorious defeat.

Based upon the communications that originated with Dog Company that night it was evident to all, that 10 platoon was engaged in the thick of the fight. It also emerged that Capt Mills, unjustifiably, as stated many times by our Colonel, at one point wanted to retreat in the face of the enemy. Levy held his ground throughout the entire battle though 10 platoon faced overwhelming odds.

To this day I cannot understand why Levy has not recognized for inspiring and leading the defence of Dog Company.

Mike Levy was married in Christ Church Cathedral, Vancouver, BC, November 1951.

E. Mel Canfield, (Retired Captain)
Private, K800112
Intelligence Section,
Battalion Headquarters Company
2nd Battalion PPCLI,
Kapyong, Korea, April 1951.

DECLARED BEFORE ME AT

A notary public in and for the
Province of British Columbia

This letter from Mel Canfield to Hub Gray describes how he overheard Colonel Jim Stone say he would not recommend Lieutenant Mike Levy for a medal at Kapyong.

Canfield, who was in the ideal position to keep track of the entire battle as it unfolded, wrote that Mills, the man who got the medal, actually "at one point wanted to retreat in the face of the enemy. Levy held his ground throughout the entire battle, even though 10 Platoon (Levy's) faced overwhelming odds."

Stone's anti-Semitic remark reflects an amazing sentiment in a no-nonsense soldier who was such a pragmatist and so prone to judge people purely on their performance and ability. No one else before or since has commented on or explained this enigmatic moment in Stone's life story.

It echoes the American Civil War general and saviour of his country, Ulysses S. Grant, who, apparently at the end of his tether under the pressures of the war, suddenly banned Jewish traders from accompanying his armies, accusing them, "as a class," of black-marketing. It was a stunning edict coming from a figure so much admired. After a word or two from Lincoln, who pointed out to Grant that he had slurred an entire religious group, many of whom were fighting in his own army, Grant rescinded the order a few days later. It was all so utterly unlike the Grant everyone knew, and the incident remains deeply puzzling after a century and a half of study. Grant later meekly said the order had been given without "due reflection," and in later years, to add to the bizarreness of it all, he appointed more Jews to public office than any other president before him.

As with the Stone-Levy-Jewish issue, it remains an enigmatic feature of a great man's makeup.

Remarkably, Levy bore not the slightest grudge against Stone, and said in later years that he would follow the man anywhere.

To add to the difficulty in understanding the baffling Stone-Levy relationship, after Kapyong he appointed Levy his Intelligence Officer, a position of great trust and confidence. A battle commander and his head of intelligence share many confidences and frankly exchange opinions, even conflicting opinions, on tactics and their fellow officers' abilities. Many who fought in the battle feel this appointment was Stone's way of apologizing to Levy for not recognizing his heroism during the battle. The whole affair still remains an unsolvable mystery sixty years later, even to Levy's family.

CHAPTER 6

JUST A WONDERFUL GROUP OF MEN

After Kapyong, the American overall commander in Korea, wary of Chinese infiltration behind his lines, decided to temporarily re-adjust the front to give his troops "breathing space," and the Patricias were pulled back slightly. And so, after everything, Kapyong was abandoned without a fight, bewildering the men who'd fought so desperately to defend it.

The next month, in May, now that the war was back on again at full throttle, the rest of the Canadian commitment, battalions of the Royal Canadian Regiment, and the French-speaking Royal 22e Régiment (the "Van Doos") began to arrive in Korea. The 2nd Battalion PPCLI, the Patricias of Kapyong, went home that November. For them, there were no parades or marching bands or flowers in the streets. It was as if no one noticed they'd been gone.

"The only thing that happened, when I came home," Don Hibbs recalls, "we landed in Vancouver and all the gangsters of the city came down to the dock and asked if we had any weapons. That was the only reception party I had."[1]

Jim Stone, who once told his troops he wouldn't be awarding them any medals because they were getting paid for what they did, was himself awarded another Distinguished Service Order (he'd already earned two others in Europe).

This rankled many of Stone's soldiers. However much they admired his courage and would have (and did) followed him through anything, this "non-medals" edict struck them as immoral. Murray

Edwards expanded on his anger in a letter that he later included in his family journal:

> Shortly after our arrival in Korea [Stone] paraded the Battalion, and wearing his DSO and Bar, MC and Bar, proceeded to tell us that since we were all volunteers and all being paid for our services, he would not be making any recommendations for individual recognition regardless of what the future held, once we were committed to action ... this was a morale-shaking shock! ... To a degree I might have accepted the Colonel's "No Recognition" policy if he had abided by his on criteria. Col. Stone failed to do so in accepting a second bar to his DSO for his own "Volunteer" service in Korea, proving himself a hypocrite.[2]

It was tough and bitter language from a loyal and competent officer who, as battalion quartermaster, was at the centre of the Kapyong fight.

Stone was so enigmatic a commander and so full of contradictions, it is difficult to get a picture of the full man.

He would say, in the 1970s to a gathering of a new generation of PPCLI officers: "Kapyong was not a great battle as battles go ... Personally I believe Kapyong was the limit of the planned offensive of the Chinese at that time. Had the limit been five miles further south, we would have been annihilated ... the numbers the Chinese were prepared to sacrifice against a position meant that eventually any unsupported battalion in defence must be over-run."[3]

Stone added that if the Chinese had persisted the outcome would have been tragically different.

And yet, in the same address where he seemed to imply it was the Chinese that lost the fight rather than the Canadians who won, he remarked: "we believed in one another and the morale of the battalion was high. No one panicked even when we knew that we were surrounded. We could have run, panicked in some way or surrendered. We stayed. We fought."

In one part of his address he would describe his Kapyong men affectionately as "adventurers," who certainly were not fighting for any grand noble cause, and were lucky to be alive after Kapyong. There was not an atom of sentimentality in Stone's makeup, but moments later in the same address, in a seemingly unguarded moment if there were such a thing with Jim Stone, he launched into a stirring and eloquent tribute to his boys.

> Their favourite marching song, had a refrain "We're untrained bums, we're from the slums."
>
> They were just a wonderful group of men. I believed in them; they believed in me. And what is more important, they believed in each other.
>
> Non professional, half-trained … they were the flesh and blood of battle.[4]

This loyalty and faith was mutual. In every army in the world, no one is a louder complainer or deeper sceptic than private soldiers. It is their lives, after all, that are at stake, and they will eternally grouse and carp about their commander's ability or the care he takes with their safety. And very often the soldiers are right. But not at Kapyong; there it was different. To a man there was, and is, a conviction that they had exactly the right man. It is impossible, even with the passing of six decades, to find any whiff of criticism of Stone's courage, professionalism, or judgement.

Even if Stone himself seemed to be not quite sure if they'd manage to hold out if the Chinese just kept on coming. His soldiers felt certain they would prevail on their hilltop simply because he was their leader.

"He knew which way was up," as one Patricia put it. "He was the brains."

So, how did it happen? How did this small band survive when the chances seemed so ridiculously small?

Arcane technical explanations of interest mainly to military analysts include: the Patricias had first-rate artillery support from the New Zealanders (not available to the Australians and the Glosters); the Chinese had outrun their own artillery; the Chinese had already expended much of their strength in driving the Aussies off their positions; the Chinese were at the end of a long communications and logistics link, stretched to its limit; the Chinese plan, fuelled by bad intelligence, was unimaginative; the Chinese were brave but showed no initiative when circumstances changed.

Then there was the Stone factor: he was a brilliant tactical commander who could "read ground." Also central to their survival was his wise (and brave) refusal to send his men into battle until they were properly trained. That decision was, literally, a lifesaver. The six-week breathing space for realistic training gave them time to develop skilful tactics as hill fighters as they worked their way up the Korean peninsula towards Hill 677, chasing guerrillas.

The Patricias gave a terrific account of themselves, but, as noted, they were also helped by a flawed and unimaginative Chinese battle plan, as noted by Major C.V. Lilley, Commander of B Company, who'd been at the centre of the fighting when the first enemy assaults fell on the Canadians:

> The Chinese telegraphed the direction and timing of their attacks by using MMG [medium machine gun] tracer ammunition for direction, sounding bugles as signals to form up on their start line and for their assault. This gave company and platoon commanders time to bring down accurate artillery, mortar and machine-gun fire on them. Before attacking in strength the Chinese did not accurately locate our defensive positions by patrolling nor did they give accurate artillery and mortar supporting fire to their troops.
>
> The steep gradients to our positions forced the Chinese to use a monkey-run attitude: in their final assault; although rifle fire in the darkness was not too effective at such small targets, grenades trundled down the hills had a devastating effect. Rocket launchers were used in an anti-personnel role and proved deadly. The Chinese appeared to be well trained and disciplined but lacked initiative. Only on orders would their squads fire their weapons or throw grenades.
>
> Their consistent attacks en masse on obvious approaches in an attempt to overwhelm our positions by sheer weight of numbers presented ideal targets for our artillery, mortars and machine-guns.[5]

The list of explanations goes on. This can get too dreamily academic and abstract; too clinical and sterile. To the private, his foxhole, at its central core of the story is not this over-analyzed detail. The simple, uncomplicated, fundamental basis of the Kapyong tale is that a small band of about 700 well-trained and highly motivated amateurs stood off an enemy of thousands of tough, seasoned professionals.

———

It seems a hopeless task to figure out the arithmetic of death at Kapyong. The amazingly low figure of ten Canadian dead and twenty-three wounded is undisputed. But the Chinese casualties are probably unknowable. The official history of the war says the Patricias and the Australians were up against 6,000 soldiers, and inflicted casualties of perhaps one third. Stone said later he would estimate Chinese dead at around 300, a figure surely far too low. William Johnson, a historian with the Department of Defence in Ottawa, puts Chinese casualties at 1,500 to 2,000. At the other end of the scale, Hub Gray, who fought at Kapyong and studied it for years afterwards, says that the Chinese had about 4,000 dead while attacking 10 Platoon alone, thanks in part to those New Zealand artillery barrages. In all, Gray calculates, the Patricias themselves inflicted at least 2,000 casualties on the enemy, and a Chinese source estimates the communist forces sustained a casualty rate of 65 percent. Historically, units cannot absorb such loss rates and remain militarily effective. Actual body counts were meaningless because the Chinese dragged away as many of their dead as they could.

Whatever the actual numbers, the men who were there argue the end result has a simple explanation. The Canadians at Kapyong, as Stone would remark, had this simple faith in themselves.

Corporal John Bishop of A Company, who later went on to become Lieutenant Colonel John Bishop and Canada's military attaché to South Korea, says they won because: "We just told ourselves, 'We are going to stay here. We are going to fight. And we're going to make it.'"[6]

So remarkable was the Patricias' stand on Kapyong, they were awarded a Presidential Unit Citation from the United States. In the five wars that Canada has fought at the side of the Americans, the 2 PPCLI remains the only Canadian unit to have won the distinction. Members wear the blue bar on their uniform to this day. Such mementos become part of the lore of the military everywhere. It is absorbed into their tradition and identity. It is the sort of invisible backup system that propels them to carry on when cold reason suggests, "Don't."

President Truman's citation was also awarded to the 3rd Battalion, Royal Australian Regiment, who fought a desperate battle on the hill next to the Patricias until they were forced off their position, and to an American armoured unit, A Company of the72nd Heavy Tank Battalion. The citation reads in part, and is probably memorized by every Patricia recruit to this day:

> Troops from a retreating division passed through the sector which enabled enemy troops to infiltrate with the withdrawing forces. The enemy attacked savagely under the clangour (sic) of bugles and trumpets. The forward elements were completely surrounded going through the first day and into the second. Again and again the enemy threw waves of troops at the outer defences, but each time the courageous, indomitable, and determined soldiers repulsed the fanatical attacks. Ammunition ran low and there was no time for food. Critical supplies were dropped by air to the encircled troops, and they stood their ground in resolute defiance of the enemy. With serene and indefatigable persistence, the gallant soldiers held their defensive positions and took heavy toll of the enemy. In some instances when the enemy penetrated the defences, the commanders directed friendly artillery fire on their own positions in repelling the thrusts. Toward the close of 25 April, the enemy break-through had been stopped. The seriousness of the break-through on the central front had been changed from defeat to victory by the gallant stand of these heroic and courageous soldiers. The 3d Battalion, Royal Australian Regiment; 2d Battalion, Princess Patricia's Canadian Light Infantry; and Company A, 72d Heavy Tank Battalion, displayed such gallantry, determination,

Photo by Hub Gray.

The wild Korean landscape with 12 Platoon dug in, sometime after Kapyong, supported by tanks of the American 72nd Heavy Tank Battalion, which also got a presidential citation for their action in the battle. The foxhole in the foreground is being defended by a Bren light machine gun, one of the few weapons the Canadians were issued that the troops had any use for.

and esprit-de-corps in accomplishing their missions under extremely difficult and hazardous conditions as to set them apart and above other units participating in the campaign, and by their achievements they brought distinguished credit on themselves, their homelands, and all freedom loving nations.

The citation was awarded in the name of the president, who as Head of State was speaking on behalf of the American people.

It is stirring stuff to have in your backpack as you head off into combat. Every Patricia patrolling in the dusts of Afghanistan must have sensed the spirits from Kapyong tromping along beside him.

Kapyong was fought in April. Truman's citation was awarded that July. But in an example of remarkable pedantry, Ottawa refused to allow the Patricias to accept the citation. The Canadian government, the Canadian Government declared, had not been asked for its permission. And there it stood for an embarrassing five years until a personal plea to Ottawa came from the Patricias' colonel-in-chief, Lady Patricia Mountbatten (daughter of the war hero, Lord Mountbatten of Burma). The citation was at last formally presented to the battalion by the American ambassador in Calgary in 1956.[7] The British and the Australian governments managed to overlook the apparent American breech of protocol, and both quickly accepted their presidential honours, but not Ottawa. The strange Canadian attitude has persisted. In a later war, Ottawa also refused to allow Canadian sniper teams in Afghanistan, who'd been protecting American troops, to accept American decorations.

Canada's Korean army came home almost unnoticed. Some soldiers stayed in service; most did not.

The 2nd Battalion was the first to go over, and the first to come home, although some like Kapyong veteran Tommy Prince, already a Second World War veteran, reenlisted and returned to the fighting. As with most veterans they were met with public indifference. Some encountered condescension from members of the Canadian Legion, who seemed to be saying Korea was no real war ... the war against the Germans, now that's what a real war is like. And so, many joined their own Korean Veterans Association where they felt more comfortable. And some joined nothing at all and put the war utterly behind them. It was not until 1992, almost a half-century after the war ended, that Ottawa finally got around to creating a Korea medal that could be worn by the men served there.

Most of the army brass at the time seemed to have learned little from Korea. One officer sneeringly told the Brigade's historian: "From the standpoint of the professional soldier with Second World War experience the lessons of the Korean War are ones that can have but limited application."[8]

This is an absurd sentiment that infuriates Korean veterans. The "professional" was certainly not who was the mainstay at Kapyong. While a few men were outstanding career soldiers, and many others, most notably Jim Stone, had been in the Second World War, it was, in essence, a citizens army that stood fast at Kapyong, not a professional one. They were, as Stone himself put it, "recruited mainly from the streets." In addition, any so-called lessons from the war against Hitler that could be applied to Korea were virtually non-existent in Korea. The terrain was strange, harsh, and alien, and so was the enemy. The lessons to be learned fighting there can well stand much study. As the Afghanistan experience has shown, "small" wars can erupt with no advance notice, in the most unlikely and unheard of places, and against people of whom we know nothing. Just like Korea.

Arguably the men of the Korean special force were the best prepared soldiers Canada had ever sent off to war anywhere; and of all the formations that ended up fighting and patrolling in the Korean hills, 2 PPCLI, the men of Kapyong, was the best led, most highly motivated, most innovative, most aggressive, and most effective. And, for the most part, when their fighting was done, they came home, quietly vanished back into civilian life, and disappeared from public memory.

Chief of the General Staff General Charles Foulkes had been uneasy from the outset with the very idea of these special force volunteers. Foulkes declared he didn't want what he called the "soldier of fortune" type in his army.

Yet, writes a modern day historian at the Department of National Defence, "it was the adventurers of these 2nd Battalions, despite their limited terms of service, who proved to be the true professionals."[9]

And it was Jim Stone who felt right from the outset the strength of his battalion was its "adventurers" who joined up precisely because there was a war on and they didn't want to miss it.

After the war, 2 PPCLI made its home in Winnipeg. The base, of course, was named Kapyong Barracks. Following a string of Department of Defence cutbacks, in 2004 the battalion was moved to Shilo, Manitoba, about a two-hour drive to the west on the open prairie, where it still is today. Kapyong Barracks was closed, abandoned, and turned over to the Canada Lands Corporation for disposal.

Over in Korea, what the Canadians did in the Kapyong Valley six decades ago remains a vivid part of local lore. Near the original battle site, the Koreans have dedicated a memorial park to what Canadians did there. For many years an aging Korean elder would participate in the Canadian veterans' services during revisit programs. He would wear gold and purple "hanbok," and the Canadian Embassy always presented him with a bottle of good scotch, wrapped in gold foil, to show respect and honour. There was also a local farmer who did the same thing, but without anyone's knowledge. He had taken refuge with his wife among the Canadians during the battle. When the North Korean troops had swept

Looking NE up the Kapyong valley, from the south, Hill 677 (Kapyong) is on the left, Australian hill is on the right. The Kapyong memorial now stands around the centre of the photo.

through the region in June, 1950, they had massacred many civilians just outside of Kapyong. The locals knew whose side those Canadians were on; their side. That farmer went to the grounds every week and pulled weeds. The site is now tended by local schoolchildren.[10]

About 27,000 Canadians served in this so-called Forgotten War before it ended in an armistice in July 1953. About 1,040 were wounded and about 520 were killed. Their bodies were not brought home, as is now the practice. They were buried near where they fell and later re-buried in the U.N. cemetery at Pusan. Canadians were killed in action before and after Kapyong, but it is Kapyong that remains the symbol of this country's fight in this far-off Asian war.

Eventually three Canadian warships were dispatched to the war. Waldo Demara, the "Great Imposter," who spent a lifetime masquerading as everything from a priest to a prison warden, spent some time in the Royal Canadian Navy serving off the coast of Korea, amazingly passing himself off as a surgeon aboard HMCS *Cayuga*. He performed many operations, successfully. Tony Curtis played Demara in the Hollywood movie.

The Royal Canadian Air Force contributed cargo planes. About twenty fighter pilots (wearing their Canadian uniforms) flew F-86 Sabres with U.S. Air Force squadrons. One flyer, Andy MacKenzie from Montreal, was shot down over MiG Alley, near the Chinese–North Korean border, and held as a POW. He was brutally treated by his captors and put up a heroic resistance against brain washing. The war had been over for a year and a half before he was finally released.

Not often mentioned in literature on the war are the 7,000 Canadians soldiers, fifty of whom were killed, who served in Korea for two years after the armistice to help police the ceasefire.

But through it all, through the three years of combat, and the more than 20,000 soldiers who fought there, it is the 700 men of Kapyong and their one-night battle alone on that hill that captures the essence of Canada in Korea.

At the time of the battle, the hillside was largely barren, covered with rocks. Low bushes and shrubs were scattered here and there. Everywhere else was desolate, with little cover; the trees had long since been used by Korean peasants for firewood.

Today, Kapyong is scarcely recognizable. The surrounding countryside is covered with a thick blanket of lush trees. The growth is so dense as to be virtually impenetrable. There is little sense of place. It could be anywhere. Most of the firing positions, scenes of such violence six decades ago, are now mostly all but gone, absorbed back into the earth and then hidden by the growth. It is not a place to wander about where visitors can try to reconstruct in their mind's eye what happened, such as at Waterloo, or Gettysburg, or Dieppe.

The location of the command headquarters is near a small road, bordered by a cornfield. There is nothing there to see. There is no way of knowing where you are. It can be reached with effort, if you know the way, but a visitor without a military historical map would never find the HQ or anything else connected with the fighting. There are no markers or signposts of any of the battle sites or platoon positions. It would be like a walk through a trailless, unmarked forest. The Kapyong memorial itself is near the bottom of Hill 677, some distance removed from where most of the fighting was. Even today, what remains so impressive still is the steepness of the Kapyong slopes.

It would take considerable stamina and fitness to climb it even now. For most veterans it is out of the question. What a murderous ordeal it must have been for those young Chinese infantrymen back then in the dark of night to scale this hill, loaded down with their burp guns and ammunition, their hearts pounding like locomotives, all the while dodging the bullets whizzing by, and artillery and mortar rounds crashing in among them, and hand grenades tumbling down the hill towards them. The Chinese must have had bad military intelligence and simply blundered into the Canadians, not realizing they were there in such strength. Or perhaps the Chinese simply underestimated the tenacity of the people they would come up against.

Many battlefields are fascinating to visit, and it's easy to grasp what happened there. They are near population centres, are expertly maintained, and offer museums, guides, guidebooks, maps, and audio/video facilities. At Gettysburg, where movements have been meticulously documented, you can retrace, literally minute-by-minute, where all the combatants were in the Civil War battle that stretched over three days. At sites such as Juno Beach, Dieppe, and Vimy Ridge, the Canadian visitor can get the feel for what it must have been like on the day. Even at Batoche in northern Saskatchewan you can still locate the rifle pits the Métis sharpshooters fired from in the final battle of their doomed struggle against the federal soldiers more than 130 years ago. In Quebec City you can scale the cliffs to the Plains of Abraham, just as James Wolfe's troops did two and a half centuries ago, and see what they saw.

But at Kapyong there is none of this. For the visitor, it is not a satisfying battlefield tour. The old company positions are separated by deep ravines, making a walkabout both exhausting and confusing. Some of the scenes of the heaviest combat, such as the spot on Kapyong's western flank where D Company and Mike Levy's 10 Platoon made their stand, are truly isolated, and higher than the other positions. It is most certainly never visited now, except by the most hale and persistent. One veteran returning in later years couldn't distinguish the Kapyong hill at all from its neighbours, let alone his old position on the hill itself. The remaining rifle pits that can still be found are not-so-slowly filling in, although

Corporal John Bishop, who returned many times during his later stint as a colonel and military attaché to Korea, could not only locate his very foxhole, but he was still proudly trim and lean enough to fit inside.

It is very quiet and tranquil at Kapyong now. For the returning veterans, this isolated serenity is the greatest and most welcome change from the most dramatic night of their lives on this spot in April 1951.

Each year the Korean government, as a gesture of thanks, hosts the return of veterans of the U.N. forces who fought to save their country. But after sixty years, their numbers dwindle. After the last Kapyong veteran passes on, it is hard to believe anyone will come to Kapyong again and explore the gullies and ravines and search out fading scars in the earth where once Canadian soldiers crouched behind the machine guns, and shouldered their rifles, and tossed hand grenades at fleeting figures in the dark, and finally fixed bayonets or swung shovels or rifle butts at the Chinese who swept into their positions. When there is no one left from Kapyong, only those Korean school children who lovingly tend the memorial park will still be there to say thank you; much as Dutch school children still remember and honour Canadians who came to help their own desperate country.

There is one remarkable Canadian who's made himself more familiar with the Kapyong battlefield than anyone anywhere today.

Ivan Duguay teaches at a South Korean university and has made a hobby of hiking and exploring the crags and gullies of Kapyong and its remote and isolated features.

With the eye of an archaeologist and the curiosity of a reporter, Duguay chronicles the ghostly scene in his many hikes over the deserted battlefield. It is a haunting record he is compiling of this vanishing landmark of Canadian history.

"It isn't a very popular mountain amongst all but the most avid hikers because it is a challenging climb, so the foxholes are better preserved than in some other battlefields I've been to … You can still find old Korean tombs that must be at least 300 years old along the slopes, so I suspect the foxholes will be visible for many more generations."

B Company's position, says Duguay, covering the Patricias' eastern flank where the first attacks fell, is the easiest to reach. Some of the foxholes here he found to be remarkably well preserved.

Directorate of History and Heritage, 681.019(D2).

Kapyong from the north.

A particularly nice one that my colleague located on the north flank of the hill is made of white stones, maybe marble, that were stacked atop one another.

We found a few .303 casings on the south side of the hill, the slope looking down on the road below, so we imagine that they had been taking shots at approaching Chinese troops as they were marching along the road several hundred metres downhill. My colleague found a light green enamel cup that appears to have been struck by a bullet or a piece of shrapnel at the bottom of this hill. There's little doubt the cup belonged to a member of the PPCLI.

… It's a huge hill. 677 isn't the highest hill we've hiked, but it is certainly has the vastest ridge lines we've tackled (it might be as much as 3km from one end of the horseshoe shaped valley to the other). I imagine it must have been an incredible demoralizing march for the Chinese soldiers because just when you think you've reached the highest peak, another one comes up behind it. It takes the better half of daylight at this time of year to reach the positions where we believe D Company were located.... It would be difficult, if not impossible, for veterans to reach D Company's positions from this path.

D Company's old position, where Mike Levy's men made their stand, is still eerily strewn with American rifle ammunition. No one knows if it had been left by Canadian soldiers using American weapons, or if the ammo had been left by Chinese soldiers using captured American weapons.

> We also found a Chinese Mauser stripper clip there. We also found the bottom part of a flare [looks like the head of a shotgun shell, but much larger] slightly behind what we believe is D Company's hill, so we wonder if PPCLI used flares to signal their positions to the planes who dropped them supplies.
>
> Slightly west to the hill we believe D Company was positioned, we found something quite astonishing: a bayonet for a Lee-Enfield rifle. A Mark 2 spike, we believe. This is where we believe PPCLI was engaged in bayonet charges or where they may have pulled back. There are foxholes dug along that particularly steep ridge, which leads straight down to the B Company's positions.
>
> What struck us mostly was the very small number of Canadian .303 casings found on those hills. Clearly, the PPCLI were very well dug in, disciplined, and accurate marksmen. They certainly weren't wasting their ammo.
>
> One of the most interesting aspects of our hobby is meeting the locals, some of which whose families have lived in the area for generations. Sometimes they offer us some incredible insights, like one particularly hospitable family who helped us locate B Company's positions. I think they see themselves as the custodians, in a sense, of the PPCLI positions. They may even own the land.

Photo by Ivan Duguay, December 2010.

A foxhole of B Company, on the Patricias' eastern flank, where the Chinese opened their assault on the surrounded Canadians. The defenders had no cover other than their quickly dug foxholes and the stones they piled around the top. The trees were not there at the time.

Local Korean villagers, he says, are knowledgeable and are happy to give directions and offer guidance.

"The Canadian memorial is well maintained … It's obvious that someone is taking care of it. It might be school kids or city employees. South Korean veterans are also quite involved in their communities, sometimes serving as caretakers and security guards at parks on a volunteer basis."

Kapyong may be the forgotten battle in the Forgotten War … but not to the people of South Korea.

The Kapyong veterans that remain are now in their eighties and nineties. Their reflections and memories are not necessarily those of the upbeat trumpeting of victors. Rather, they are often curiously melancholy, thinking of those left behind and who will remain forever young.

Bill White doesn't go to re-unions and has never returned to Korea. "I would only go back to see a couple of my buddies, in the cemetery."[11]

Kim Reynolds scarcely thinks of Korea at all today. He too has never gone back. He says. "I got on with my life."[12]

Bill Chrysler, though, developed a great fondness for Korea, fell in love with the country and its people, and also fell in love with, and married, a Korean. But he deliberately made few friends in the Patricias and he is very private with his memories: "Sometimes my wife sees a tear running down my cheek. I made it a habit never to get close to anyone in the war. I couldn't bear to lose a friend so I didn't know anyone. I kept my distance. There were a lot of nice guys there, but to protect my feelings I didn't want to get too friendly with them."[13]

Then there's the irrepressible, un-put-down-able Smiley Douglas, who lost a hand trying to save his men when a live grenade landed in their midst. He is now is in his eighties and still lives on his Alberta farm. He remains as delightful and as upbeat as ever. He keeps his medal "in a cupboard somewhere" and rarely wears it. He holds no grudges against the enemy, whom he describes as "some poor old Chinese guys doing exactly the same job I was doing; doing what they were told." He has not an ounce of bitterness about losing his hand. "What the hell. It could have been my head. Then I'd have had nothing to worry about." And the war? "It was probably the best time I had in my life."[14]

And Don Hibbs, who has a thousand memories from Kapyong, keeps it all in perspective and refuses to be philosophic: "Aw, it's just a hill, after all. Just like thousands of other hills over there. It's just a hill."[15]

The final, saddest, and most poignant reflection on the Patricias' stand on that hill surely belongs to Bob Menard, who helped recover the dead when the shooting subsided slightly.

When he came to the bodies of the slain men, he discovered no one had died singly or alone. They went down in little groups of two.

"They died in their foxholes," says Menard, speaking ever so slowly now, and pausing to collect his thoughts.

"They'd gone down fighting. We always found them, two together. They were defending each other to the very end."[16]

Whatever Happened to ...

In July 1951, peace talks began, then broke off in August, and sputtered along on and off until the final armistice in 1953. That fall, 2 PPCLI, our first Korean army, came home and other troops were rotated in.

There are no precise or official statistics, but the sense among veterans is that perhaps 60 percent of the Kapyong Patricias, the soldiers in this citizen's army, quietly returned to where they began it all — to civilian life — and vanished from history.

Mackenzie King died June 22, 1950, ever wary about any involvement in Korea. Sixteen days later Prime Minister Louis St. Laurent announced Canada would send a special force to fight there.

Matthew Ridgway, commander of all forces in South Korea and one of the most distinguished figures in American military history, retired from the Army in 1955. He later advised Lyndon Johnson against deeper involvement in Vietnam. In 1971, his son was killed in a canoeing accident near in northern Ontario. His ashes were scattered over the Canadian Shield. Ridgway died in 1993. Colin Powell delivered the graveside eulogy.

Douglas MacArthur, one of the most brilliant, charismatic, and erratic commanders in U.S. history, was fired by President Truman in April 1951 for insubordination. His biographer called him an "American Caesar." He died in 1964, having cautioned presidents Kennedy and Johnson against a build-up in Vietnam. He was a great student of history and much admired James Wolfe's campaign at Quebec. After Kapyong, MacArthur said that 2 PPCLI had done "a great job in that fight."

John Rockingham, the commanding officer of the Canadian troops in Korea, retired much-decorated from the Army in 1966, one of the most battle-savvy senior officers ever produced by the Canadian army. He died in 1987.

Jim Stone, the fighting Commanding Officer of 2 PPCLI at Kapyong, after the war went on to become a parachutist (in his forties!), and commanded the Mobile Striking Force, the forerunner of the Airborne Regiment. In 1953 he was a appointed chief instructor at the Royal Canadian School of Infantry, at Camp Borden, just north of Toronto. Later, he commanded the Army's Provost Corps, the military police. The day after Kapyong, Stone was informed his daughter had eye cancer, which took her life soon after. Stone then helped found the Military Police Fund For Blind Children, which has raised millions of dollars for equipment, training guide dogs, and recreation. Stone described it as "the greatest accomplishment of my life." He died in 2005 in Victoria. He was ninety-seven. Everyone he met or served with regarded Stone as a superb combat commander.

Mike Levy, the heroic commander of 10 Platoon, made the army his career, and his missions abroad included assignments in Germany, Cyprus, and the International Commission in Vietnam. He attended the U.S. Marine Corps Command and Staff College and retired in 1974 with the rank of major. Like Stone, Levy was a complete soldier. He died in Vancouver in 2007. A man of great modesty and stirring personal leadership, his bravery and integrity was the stuff of legend throughout the army.

Ken Barwise, of D Company, decorated for his bravery at Kapyong, stayed in the army until he retired. He died in 2008.

Wayne Mitchell, also decorated for bravery, died in 1999.

Captain Wally Mills, the decorated commander of D Company, died in 1995.

John Diefenbaker, the flamboyant lawyer who defended the railway telegrapher accused of being responsible for the derailing of the troop train as it went through the Rockies, became prime minister in 1957. He once told the author that the acquittal of the poor telegrapher was easily his most satisfying courtroom victory. Diefenbaker died in 1979.

Tommy Prince, the Manitoba Ojibwe and Devil's Brigade veteran from the Second World War, served in A Company at Kapyong. In Korea he became famous for his night "snatch" patrols and was eventually given fewer such assignments because he took too many risks. Prince unbelievably volunteered for a second tour in Korea, returning with the 3rd Battalion of the PPCLI, where he again distinguished himself with much heroism and was wounded. Sadly, Tommy Prince lived out his final years alone in a Salvation Army hostel in Winnipeg. He had sold off his medals to support himself. The author met and interviewed him in the early 1970s. Prince died in poverty in 1977.

Bill Chrysler, the machine gunner from Fort Erie, Ontario, who helped save the command post from being overrun at Kapyong, went back to Korea briefly after the war to work in construction. As a souvenir, he kept part of the parachute used in the American airdrop, then years later he finally threw it away. He says now: "I've kicked my ass ever since."

Hub Gray, whose book on Mike Levy's role at Kapyong brought the neglected hero in from the shadows, lives in retirement in Calgary and is contemplating a book about his own father, Charles Frederick Gray, who was mayor of Winnipeg during the General Strike.

Murray Edwards stayed in the army until he retired in 1969 as a major. He became a teacher.

Kim Reynolds was an electrician when he joined the army, and he became one again when he left.

Wally Lapoint, a highway surveyor, took a sniper course after Kapyong and stayed in the army another three years after Korea.

Mike Melnechuck, who took home movies at Kapyong, which later vanished, was a Second World War veteran who stayed in the army and retired as a warrant officer. He died in 2010.

Al Lynch stayed in the army and transferred to the Queen's Own Rifles.

Mike Czuboka, who lied about his age to join up, became a teacher and high school principal in Manitoba and wrote several books, including one on the Ukrainian experience in Canada.

Don Hibbs, the ebullient cab driver from Guelph, who regretted missing out on the Second World War, stayed on in the Army, retired as a sergeant, and became an insurance broker.

Alex Sim, one of the first to come under fire at Kapyong, remained in the Army until 1969 when he retired as a warrant officer and then worked in occupational health.

Charles Petrie, who also served in the Second World War, was a platoon commander in the beleaguered B Company, stayed in the army until 1970, and retired as captain to teach in the U.K.

Gordon Henderson, the battle adjutant who was so puzzled by the conduct of Wally Mills during the battle, died in 2009.

Rod Middleton, who was almost killed leading attacks on Hill 532 and then offered to lead yet another attack in place of an exhausted Mike Levy, retired from the army as a major and remained active in many PPCLI museums and organizations. He died in 2005.

Mel Canfield, the private in an intelligence section who was logging radio communications during the battle and overheard Stone's remark about Levy, retired from the army in 1973 with the rank of captain. He died in 2009.

Jack James, the United Press International reporter whose international scoop broke the story on the North Korean invasion, died in 2000. He was seventy-nine.

And finally, the tired, friendless, dilapidated troopship, USS *Private Joe P. Martinez*, that carried the Patricias off to war in 1950, was also assigned to take the same horrified troops back home when their tour of duty was over. Some soldiers refused to board, and sensibly were not court-martialled for their defiance. The *Martinez* was retired from service by the U.S. Navy in 1951, mothballed, and finally scrapped in 1971. It was an unlamented passing.

DECORATIONS WON AT KAPYONG

These five medals were all won for combat in a time span lasting about twelve hours:

Colonel Jim Stone, Distinguished Service Order (bar). A "bar" is awarded when a soldier has already won the decoration in a previous action. At Kapyong, Stone's bar was in fact his third DSO. His first DSO and subsequent bar were awarded for his exploits in the Second World War.

Captain Wally Mills, Military Cross. Mills was the commanding officer of D Company which was shelled by its own artillery to prevent it from being overrun.

Private Wayne Mitchell, Distinguished Conduct Medal, second only to the Victoria Cross. Mitchell, though repeatedly wounded, blazed away single-handedly at enemy soldiers with his machine gun to prevent his position with B Company from being overrun.

Lance Corporal Smiley Douglas, Military Medal. Douglas lost a hand trying to dispose of a live hand grenade that had fallen among his B Company platoon. Two weeks later, CBC Radio broadcast a brief interview: *archives.cbc.ca/war_conflict/korean_war/clips/732/.*

Private Ken Barwise, Military Medal. He is credited with killing six enemy soldiers "at very close range," recaptured a machine gun and ran a gauntlet of heavy fire to deliver ammunition to hard pressed 10 Platoon (Mike Levy's) in D Company.

KILLED IN ACTION AT KAPYONG

Private M.S. Carr, 24, D Company, 12 Platoon

Corporal C.R. Evans, 23, B Company, 6 Platoon

Private L.T. Fielding, 23, B Company, 6 Platoon

Private C.A. Hayes, 21, B Company, 6 Platoon

Private J.M. Lessard, 23, D Company, 12 Platoon

Private B.M. MacDonald, 20, D Company, 12 Platoon

Private W.J. Marshall, 22, D Company, 12 Platoon

Private R.G.H. Tolver, 26, B Company, 6 Platoon

Private R.L. Walker, 23, Pioneer (engineering) Platoon

Private T.B. Wotton, 22, D Company, 11 Platoon

NOTES

INTRODUCTION

1. Speech by Colonel Jim Stone to officers of 3 PPCLI. The Military Museums Library and Archives, University of Calgary, Libraries and Cultural Resources (December 18, 1973). Gift of Hub Gray.
2. Jack Granatstein, interview with the author, August 2010.
3. David Bercuson, interview with the author, August 2010.

CHAPTER 1: CANADA IS NOT SIR GALAHAD

1. "Reds Rip Gaping Hole in UN Line," *Globe and Mail* (April 24, 1951,): 1.
2. J.W. Pickersgill and D.F. Forster, *The Mackenzie King Record, Volume 4* (Toronto: University of Toronto Press, 1970), 134.

CHAPTER 2: JACK JAMES'S SCOOP

1. R. R. Keene, "The Korean War: It Started on A Sunday in June," *Leatherneck Magazine* (June 2010): *www.mca-marines.org/ leatherneck/article/korean-war-it-started-sunday-june*.
2. Mark Zuehlke, *Ortona: Canada's Epic World War II Battle* (Vancouver: Douglas & McIntyre, 1999). Mark Zuehlke website: *www.zuehlke.ca/Excerpts/ortona*.

3. "Big Jim From Ortona Rejoins The Army; Canada's 'Legend' To Head Unit In Korea," *Winnipeg Free Press* (August 16, 1950): 10.

4 Speech by Colonel Jim Stone to officers of 3 PPCLI. The Military Museums Library and Archives, University of Calgary, Libraries and Cultural Resources (December 18, 1973). Gift of Hub Gray.

5. *Ibid.*

6. Pierre Berton, *Maclean's* (June 21, 2003).

7. Don Hibbs, interview with the author, February 2008.

8. John Bishop, interview with the author, February 2008.

9. Alex Sim, interview with the author, May 2010.

10. Mike Czuboka, interview with the author, February 2008.

11. *Ibid.*

12. John Bishop, *The King's Bishop* (Duncan, B.C.: Mossy Knoll Enterprises, 2000), 33.

13. Smiley Douglas, interview with the author, February 2008.

Chapter 3: A Citizen's Army Goes To War

1. Al Lynch, interview with the author, February 2008.

2. Letter from Jim Stone to Professor David Bercuson. The Military Museums Library and Archives, University of Calgary, Libraries and Cultural Resources (December 5, 1999). Gift of Hub Gray

3. *Ibid.*

4. John Bishop, interview with the author, February 2008.

5. Mike Czuboka, interview with the author, February 2008.

6. John Bishop, interview with the author.

7. Mike Czuboka, interview with the author.

8. Al Lynch, interview with the author.

9. Mike Czuboka, interview with the author.

10. *Ibid.*

11. Don Hibbs, interview with the author, February 2008.

12. Bill Chrysler, interview with the author, May 2010.

13. John Melady, *Korea: Canada's Forgotten War* (Toronto: Macmillan of Canada, 1983), 64.

14. Murray Edwards, interview with the author, February 2008.
15. Alex Sim, interview with the author, May 2010.
16. Murray Edwards, private memoirs, Album One, 12.
17. *Ibid.*
18. Murray Edwards, 13.
19. *2 PPCLI War Diary*, Library and Archives Canada, RG 24, Vol 18, (16 and 17 January, 1951), 317.
20. Murray Edwards, 28–29.
21. *Ibid.*
22. *Ibid.*
23. Murray Edwards, 44.

CHAPTER 4: DEATH IN THE SNOW

1. Kim Reynolds, interview with the author, May 2010.
2. Mike Czuboka, interview with the author, February 2008.
3. Murray Edwards, private memoirs, Album One, 17.
4. Alex Sim, interview with the author, May 2010.
5. John Bishop, *The King's Bishop* (Duncan, B.C.: Mossy Knoll Enterprises, 2000), 50.
6. Don Hibbs, interview with the author, February 2008.
7. *Ibid.*
8. John Bishop, interview with the author, February 2008.
9. Al Lynch, interview with the author, February 2008.
10. *Ibid.*
11. Bill Chrysler, interview with the author, May 2010.
12. Kim Reynolds, interview with the author.
13. John Bishop, interview with the author.
14. Kim Reynolds, interview with the author.
15. Pierre Berton, *Maclean's* (June 1, 1951).
16. Herbert Fairlie Wood, *Strange Battleground: The Operations in Korea and Their Effects on the Defence Policy of Canada* (Ottawa: Queen's Printer, 1966), 71.
17. John Bishop, *The King's Bishop*, 55.
18. *Ibid.*, 56.

19. *Ibid.*, 57.
20. *Calgary Herald* (March 5, 1951).
21. "Notes on Fighting in Korea," Department of National Defence, Directory of History and Heritage, Ottawa, file 314.009 (D464) (April 23, 1951).
22. Don Hibbs, interview with the author.
23. John Bishop, interview with the author.
24. Mike Czuboka, interview with the author.
25. Hub Gray, *Beyond the Danger Close: The Korean Experience Revealed: 2nd Battalion Princess Patricia's Canadian Light Infantry* (Calgary: Bunker to Bunker Publishing, 2003), 25.
26. John Bishop, *The King's Bishop*, 76.
27. *Ibid.*, 77.
28. *Ibid.*
29. William Johnson, *A War of Patrols: A War of Patrols: Canadian Army Operations in Korea* (Vancouver: UBC Press, 2003), 75.
30. Hub Gray, *Beyond the Danger Close*, 26.
31. *Ibid.*, 27.
32. *Ibid.*
33. Robert Hepenstall, *Find the Dragon: The Canadian Army in Korea, 1950–1953* (Edmonton: Four Winds Publishing, 1995), 77.
34. Don Hibbs, interview with the author.
35. William Johnson, *A War of Patrols*, 78.
36. *Ibid.*
37. John Melady, *Korea: The Forgotten War* (Toronto: Macmillan of Canada, 1983), 70.
38. Hub Gray, *Beyond the Danger Close*, 186.
39. *Ibid.*, 187.
40. *Ibid.*, 247.
41. *Ibid.*, 248.
42. *Ibid.*, 249.
43. Murray Edwards, private memoirs, Album Two, 1.
44. Hub Gray, *Beyond the Danger Close*, 51.
45. Alex Sim, interview with the author.

CHAPTER 5: THE BATTLE BEGINS: "LET THE BASTARDS COME!"

1. William Johnson, *A War of Patrols: A War of Patrols: Canadian Army Operations in Korea* (Vancouver: UBC Press, 2003), 93.
2. Hub Gray, *Beyond the Danger Close: The Korean Experience Revealed: 2nd Battalion Princess Patricia's Canadian Light Infantry* (Calgary: Bunker to Bunker Publishing, 2003), 228.
3. Mike Czuboka, interview with the author, February 2008.
4. Murray Edwards, interview with the author, February 2008.
5. Hub Gray, *Beyond the Danger Close*, 61.
6. Captain Owen Browne, *The Patrician*, no. 20 (Edmonton, 1967), 19.
7. Bill Chrysler, interview with the author, May 2010.
8. Alex Sim, interview with the author, May 2010.
9. Hub Gray, *Beyond the Danger Close*, 73.
10. Captain Owen Browne, *The Patrician*, no. 20 (Edmonton, 1967), 20.
11. Bill White, interview with the author, February 2008.
12. *Ibid.*
13. Charles Petrie, interview with the author, February 2008.
14. Alex Sim, interview with the author.
15. Murray Edwards, interview with the author.
16. Smiley Douglas, interview with the author, February 2008.
17. Murray Edwards, interview with the author.
18. Bill Chrysler, interview with the author.
19. Murray Edwards, interview with the author.
20. Don Hibbs, interview with the author, February 2008.
21. Hub Gray, *Beyond the Danger Close*, 83.
22. Mike Czuboka, interview with the author.
23. John Bishop, interview with author, February 2008.
24. *Ibid.*
25. Alex Sim, interview with the author.
26. Don Hibbs, interview with the author.
27. Murray Edwards, interview with the author.
28. Kim Reynolds, interview with the author, May 2010.
29. Don Hibbs, interview with the author.
30. Alex Sim, interview with the author.

31. Kim Reynolds, interview with the author.
32. Charles Petrie, interview with the author.
33. Al Lynch, interview with the author, February 2008.
34. Hub Gray, *Beyond the Danger Close*, 230.
35. *Ibid.*
36. Kim Reynolds, interview with the author.
37. Alex Sim, interview with the author.
38. Hub Gray, *Beyond the Danger Close*, 238.
39. *Ibid.*
40. Bob Menard, interview with author
41. Smiley Douglas, interview with the author.
42. Charles Petrie, interview with the author.
43. Captain Owen Browne, *The Patrician*, no. 20 (Edmonton, 1967), 21.
44. Hub Gray, *Beyond the Danger Close*, 91.
45. Bill Chrysler, interview with the author.
46. Mike Czuboka, interview with the author.
47. Bill Chrysler, interview with the author.
48. Hub Gray, *Beyond the Danger Close*, 93.
49. *Ibid.*
50. Mike Czuboka, interview with the author.
51. Bill White, interview with the author.
52. Robert Hepenstall, *Find the Dragon* (Edmonton: Four Winds Publishing, 1995), 96.
53. Charles Petrie, interview with the author.
54. Statement of Lieutenant Michael Levy. The Military Museums Library and Archives, University of Calgary, Libraries and Cultural Resources (October 17, 1997). Gift of Hub Gray.
55. PPCLI Archives, Calgary.
56. *Ibid.*
57. Hub Gray, *Beyond the Danger Close*, 106.
58. PPCLI Archives, Calgary.
59. Herbert Fairlie Wood, *Strange Battleground: The Operations in Korea and Their Effects on the Defence Policy of Canada* (Ottawa: Queen's Printer, 1966), 88.
60. Private interview with the author, May 2010.

61. Gordon Henderson letter to Hub Gray. The Military Museums Library and Archives, University of Calgary, Libraries and Cultural Resources (June 3, 1998). Gift of Hub Gray.

62. *Ibid.*

63. Transcript of a conversation between Mike Levy and Hub Gray. The Military Museums Library and Archives, University of Calgary, Libraries and Cultural Resources (October 25, 2007). Gift of Hub Gray.

64. *Ibid.*

65. Murray Edwards, interview with the author.

66. Mike Czuboka, interview with the author.

67. John Bishop, interview with the author.

68. Don Hibbs, interview with the author.

69. Bill Chrysler, interview with the author.

70. Don Hibbs, interview with the author.

71. Al Lynch, interview with the author.

72. Bill White, interview with the author.

73. Alex Sim, interview with the author.

74. *Ibid.*

75. John Bishop, interview with the author.

76. Don Hibbs, interview with the author.

77. Bill Chrysler, interview with the author.

78. Rollie Lapointe, interview with the author, May 2010.

79. Notes kindly supplied to author by Charles Petrie.

80. Bob Menard, interview with author, May 2010.

81. Mel Canfield letter to Hub Gray. The Military Museums Library and Archives, University of Calgary, Libraries and Cultural Resources (April 2, 2002). Gift of Hub Gray.

Chapter 6: Just a Wonderful Group of Men

1. Don Hibbs, interview with the author, February 2008.

2. Murray Edwards, private memoirs, Album One, 74.

3. Speech by Colonel Jim Stone to officers of 3 PPCLI. The Military Museums Library and Archives, University of Calgary, Libraries and Cultural Resources (December 18, 1973). Gift of Hub Gray.

4. *Ibid.*

5. Herbert Fairlie Wood, *Strange Battleground* (Ottawa, Queen's Printer, 1966), 89.

6. John Bishop, interview with the author, February 2008.

7. Murray Edwards, interview with the author, February 2008. Edwards was appointed aide to the U.S. ambassador for the presentation ceremony.

8. Brent Byron Watson, *Far Eastern Tour* (Montreal and Kingston, McGill-Queen's University Press, 2002) 178

9. William Johnson, *A War of Patrols* (Vancouver, UBCPress, 2003), 376.

10. Information kindly provided by Vince Courtenay

11. Bill White, interview with the author, February 2008.

12. Kim Reynolds, interview with the author, May 2010.

13. Bill Chrysler, interview with the author, May 2010.

14. Smiley Douglas, interview with the author, February 2008.

15. Don Hibbs, interview with the author.

16. Bob Menard, interview with the author, May 2010.

Further Reading

With one exception, little has been written on Kapyong itself. Most works mention the battle only in passing while examining the overall course of the war.

Barris, Ted. *Deadlock in Korea: Canadians at War, 1950–1953.* Toronto: Macmillan Canada, 1999. This is a good popular overall account of Canada's war in Korea, covering all three services and the little-discussed story of Canadian POWs held by the Chinese.

Bercuson, David. *Blood on the Hills: The Canadian Army in the Korean War.* Toronto: University of Toronto Press, 1999. A well-written study of Canada's war in Korea by one of the country's leading military scholars. It is critical of Canadian training and weapons (though not by-and-large of the troops themselves) and of the lessons not learned.

Bishop, John R. *The King's Bishop.* Duncan, B.C.: Mossy Knoll Enterprises, 2000. An engaging personal account of a young soldier's first months in Korea and then at Kapyong.

Gray, Hub. *Beyond the Danger Close: The Korean Experience Revealed: 2nd Battalion Princess Patricia's Canadian Light Infantry.* Calgary: Bunker to Bunker Publishing, 2003. This is a remarkable minute-by-minute account of Kapyong from a man who was there.

Hastings, Max. *The Korean War.* London: Pan Books, 1988. A good study by a leading British military historian, with emphasis on Commonwealth troops in the war

Johnson, William. *A War of Patrols: Canadian Army Operations in Korea*. Vancouver: UBC Press, 2003. This is a wide-ranging study by an historian at the Directorate of History and Heritage, Department of National Defence. Johnson argues the first Canadian troops in Korea, 2 PPCLI, were probably the most effective.

Manchester William. *American Caesar: Douglas MacArthur 1880–1964*. London: Little Brown, 1978. This is a classic biography, still unsurpassed after more than thirty years, and also a wonderful work of literature.

Melady, John. *Korea: Canada's Forgotten War*. Toronto: Macmillan of Canada, 1983. This is one of the earliest popular works on Canada on the Korean War. Written almost three decades ago, but stands up surprising well.

Pickersgill, Jack and D.F. Forster. *The Mackenzie King Record, Volume 4: 1947–1948*. Toronto: University of Toronto Press, 1970. This is the closest look we'll get inside the mind of Canada's quirky, quixotic, and surprisingly wise prime minister who was wary of anything to do with entanglements in Korea.

Watson, Brent Byron. *Far Eastern Tour: The Canadian Infantry in Korea, 1950–1953*. Montreal and Kingston: McGill-Queen's University Press, 2002. This is a good study of issues other than combat, such as cooking, casualties, and defensive attitude of troops in the war's latter stages.

Wood, Herbert Fairlie. *Strange Battleground: The Operations in Korea and Their Effects on the Defence Policy of Canada*. Ottawa: Queen's Printer, 1966. It is available on the internet at: *www.cmp-cpm.forces.gc.ca/dhh-dhp/his/docs/Battlegrd_e.pdf*.

The Korean Veterans Association of Canada maintains a vast website at *www.kvacanada.com/canadians_in_the_korean_war.htm*, with many articles, photographs, memoirs, and links.

The PPCLI itself maintains an extensive website at *www.ppcli.com*, with background on the history on the various battalions, and battle honours from the First World War to Afghanistan. The PPCLI Museum and Archives in Calgary is the Regiment's repository of thousands of photographs, letters, diaries, newspaper clippings, books, and other related documents, including the PPCLI's own War Diaries. The museum also has on display a vivid diorama of Kapyong.

INDEX

Of Related Interest

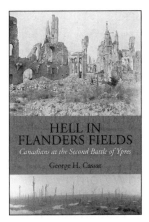

Hell in Flanders Fields
Canada at the Second Battle of Ypres
by George H. Cassar
978-1554887286
$36.00

On April 22, 1915, the men of the 1st Canadian Division faced chlorine gas. In defiance of a particularly horrible death, these untested Canadians fought almost continuously for four days, often hand-to-hand, as they clung stubbornly against overwhelming odds to a vital part of the Allied line after the French units on their left fled in panic. By doing so, they saved fifty thousand troops in the Ypres salient from almost certain destruction, and prevented the momentum of the war from tipping in favour of the Germans. In this deeply researched account, George H. Cassar skillfully blends into the history of the battle the graphic and moving words of the men on the front line. *Hell in Flanders Fields* is an authoritative, gripping drama of politics, strategy, and human courage.

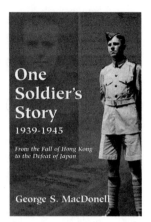

One Soldier's Story: 1939–1945
From the Fall of Hong Kong to the Defeat of Japan
by George S. MacDonell
978-1550024081
$19.99

This is the story of a seventeen-year-old boy who ran away from home to join the Canadian Army at the outbreak of the Second World War in 1939. It describes the fateful adventures of two regiments dispatched to the Pacific to face the Japanese, and the courage of two thousand young soldiers who, when faced with an impossible task thousands of miles from home, behaved with honour and distinction. Though they lost the battle of Hong Kong, they succeeded in showing the world the mettle of which they were made.

Available at your favourite bookseller.

What did you think of this book?
Visit www.dundurn.com for reviews, videos, updates, and more!